KARL M. KAPP

ROBYN A. DEFELICE

MICROLEARNING

SHORT AND SWEET

ATD Press is an internationally renowned source of insightful and practical information on
talent development, training, and professional development.

ATD Press
1640 King Street
Alexandria, VA 22314 USA

Ordering information: Books published by ATD Press can be purchased by visiting ATD's
website at www.td.org/books or by calling 800.628.2783 or 703.683.8100.

Library of Congress Control Number: 2019945544

ISBN-10: 1-949036-73-1
ISBN-13: 978-1-949036-73-2
e-ISBN: 978-1-949036-74-9

ATD Press Editorial Staff
Director: Sarah Halgas
Manager: Melissa Jones
Community of Practice Manager, Learning Technologies: Justin Brusino
Developmental Editor: Jack Harlow
Text Design: Michelle Jose and Shirley E.M. Raybuck
Cover Design: Faceout Studio, Spencer Fuller
Printed by Data Reproductions Corporation, Auburn Hills, MI

Contents

Foreword v

Acknowledgments ix

Section 1. Foundations 1

    1. What Is Microlearning? 3

    2. Learning Principles and Microlearning 21

    3. Uses of Microlearning 41

    4. How to Put Microlearning Into Action 55

Section 2. Planning & Development 69

    5. Creating a Microlearning Strategy 71

    6. Planning and Implementing Microlearning 89

    7. Designing Microlearning 109

    8. Measuring the Effectiveness of Microlearning 137

Conclusion 157

References 171

About the Authors 177

Index 181

Foreword

Why We Wrote This Book

At first, the notion of writing a book on microlearning was a bit preposterous. Shouldn't we just apply the microlearning concept we are writing about to develop the material? After all, isn't a book something you sit down and read over the course of several hours? If you had to make the comparison, that feels more like a full-length training program. Why wouldn't we chunk the content into tiny portions, convert to PowerPoint slides, add some narration, and post it online? Isn't that what microlearning is all about?

Well, to be honest, no. That's why we decided a book was needed to demystify what microlearning really is, to offer all the learning theories and research that support it, and to present an actionable road map for planning, implementing, designing, and evaluating it.

All learning approaches need defined foundations, valid theory and research to support the method, and a look at the development process from analysis through to evaluation. We know microlearning is trending, and many are enthusiastic to adopt it. However, we also get that not everyone knows how or why to use microlearning. And even more important is to ask, should they?

Today, there is little that provides the comprehensive background necessary to make informed training design decisions about microlearning. In doing our research, we found nuggets of great information on the topic, but not a comprehensive guidebook to assist in making those efforts actionable.

We wouldn't implement an entirely new approach to learning without doing the upfront research or perhaps a pilot to determine its value for our organization or client. Why would you do that with microlearning? That's why we wrote this book, to provide that beginning for you.

Microlearning may seem like just another item to put in the instructional designer's (ID's) toolkit; use sound instructional design practices, plan the initiative, and off you go! However, that method may only work for a small minority of IDs. With any learning approach, there are nuances you must recognize because they alter our standard methods of developing learning. Microlearning is no different.

For example, the idea that microlearning is a quick and easy way to jazz up a stale learning program is a bit of a myth. Microlearning can actually take just as long, if not more time, to develop and implement. This is because microlearning is typically distributed over a period of time. If that's not what your organization does for standard implementation, it may woefully underestimate the resources necessary for executing the solution. It's not always as simple as uploading a program into a learning management system (LMS) and providing notice of a new course. It could take time every week, month, or business quarter to create and launch the microlearning initiative your organization created.

What we are saying is that microlearning needs as much attention from an instructional design standpoint as any other form of training. Keeping this in mind will help keep microlearning from being another "learning trend" your company attempted to adopt but failed. If this has happened, we hope this book provides the confidence you need to give microlearning a much deserved second try!

The Best Way to Read This Book

Microlearning: Short and Sweet is designed to accommodate the novice through to the pros. The practical approach to the topics provides an opportunity to pick and choose what you need to answer your most immediate questions on the subject—or to dive deeper to gain a more comprehensive understanding.

No matter your level of familiarity with microlearning concepts, we encourage all readers to start with chapter 1. We not only provide examples of microlearning, but we dive into what microlearning is and is not to help clear up any misconceptions. Additionally, we've compiled several definitions of what microlearning is and developed a common set of characterizations that allowed us to operationalize a standard definition. Reviewing this chapter first, whether you're tenured in training development or new to the topic, ensures that as you read other chapters you have the appropriate context.

Now, from there it depends on what you are seeking to know or do. If you are a traditionalist in reading books, the layout of the chapters provides a logical path through the subject matter. Chapter 2 digs into the learning theory and domains that microlearning complements. Chapter 3 highlights the use cases of microlearning. Then, chapter 4 offers a primer on microlearning from a "why it works and when to use it" perspective. Having an idea of what you are hoping to teach, train, develop, and so on in the back of your head while you read these chapters will help you visualize which principles and practices will work best for your subject matter.

Chapters 5, 6, 7, and 8 get to the "hands dirty" part of microlearning: creating, designing, implementing, and evaluating microlearning products. To help elaborate the key concepts of each chapter, we have woven in case studies that were generously shared by peers leading the way in microlearning. There are a lot of folks out there doing great things with microlearning, and each case exemplifies points we make throughout the book.

With each of these chapters we look at the design and development process, not only from its impact on the learner, but also its impact on the learning developer. Our years in the field have taught us that we must be realists about what we can do as learning development professionals, given the organizational constraints and interdependencies we're presented with. We want the best for our learners, but as the developers, we know we must work under certain constraints.

We conclude the book with a recap of the key takeaways from each chapter and then take a brief look at what the future may have in store for microlearning design and development.

We hope this book fuels your creative mind to see the endless possibilities for microlearning in your organization.

Acknowledgments

Karl: All good work is built upon the shoulders of others. In that spirit, I'd like to thank the pioneers who have written and presented extensively on the subject of microlearning, helping to shape the field in that area and guide some of my thinking about microlearning. Those folks include Carla Torgerson, JD Dillon, Shannon Tipton, Will Thalheimer, and Clark Quinn. I know there are others whom I have probably forgotten, but thanks to all those great folks. Also, thanks to Tim Wikstrom who supplied a case study about Presentr, to JD who provided the Axonify case study, and to Jordan Fladell for information on the mLevel microlearning piece early in the book. Thanks to Clark Aldrich for his work on short sim; he is always a step ahead. Also, a huge shout out to the folks at Gameffective, who provided a great case study. And, thanks to Tal Valler whom I work with on an almost daily basis discussing microlearning and some form of gamification. Also, to the wonderful team at iLookout, which is implementing microlearning in an intelligent and meaningful way.

A special thanks to Kristine Luecker who got this book started, to Jack Harlow who carefully and masterfully shepherded the book to completion, and to Justin Brusino for his continued support of the field and of new and exciting ideas in learning and development (he at least always listens to my crazy ideas). And to Melissa Jones for her help in making our prose sound great.

To my wife, Nancy, who is nothing short of wonderful; my two boys (Nate and Nick), whom I love and cherish; my mother, who taught me to love learning; and my late father, who taught me the value of hard work.

I'd like to thank the folks in Bloomsburg University's Department of Instructional Technology and the dean of our college. I couldn't ask to work with better faculty, staff, or administrators. Special thanks to the students in the program, and to students everywhere whom I've had the honor and privilege of teaching and who have taught me much as well. Teaching is a wonderful two-way street.

Finally, a huge acknowledgment and thank you to Robyn Defelice! Her hard work in the face of adversity, her diligence, and her strength are remarkable. I am proud to know her as a student, as a colleague, and as a friend. Thanks Robyn.

Robyn: How do you follow that? Well, with echoing Karl's appreciation and gratitude for contributions, such as Tamer Ali for the ASCME case study and Amy Loomis for her insights on microlearning and digital learning environments.

Not to mention the fine folks at ATD, like Jack Harlow, our editor. I really appreciated Jack's enthusiasm for the subject and collaborating with us to shape the book. Definitely need to agree with Karl on Justin; he appreciates (I think) my excitement for data and my desire to share practical advice with our field!

My roots are not only with Bloomsburg University and the Department of Instructional Technology, but also with Indiana University of Pennsylvania. Both educational institutions have been a large part of my professional and personal development. In addition, my interest in microlearning emerged at LaSalle University and has been supported as part of my teaching approach there.

From a more personal side, it's really my macro circle of family and friends that need the most thanks. So, Sean, Sally, my late father, Mom, Jamie, Krista, Vinny, Brittney, PJ, Carla, Lonny, and Meredith, thank you for the incredible support and laughter! Not to mention: Macy, Javin, Alec, Landyn, Carmen, Levi, Michael, and Maveryk—they are microlessons in life and I love every minute of how they inspire me!

What's even more awesome is for different moments and moods I have micro-relations within that circle that keep me going with my endeavors and ambitions! There are too many to list, but they have listened willingly (most of the time) to me "nerd out" or encouraged me to keep going when I had doubt.

However, no one has ever really been able to tame the incessant four-year-old in me—who asks 100 "whys?" about the field of learning and development—more than Karl. I've enjoyed our collegial research, contributing to your classes, and supporting each other's professional passions. Thanks for listening to my crazy ideas as well! Grazie mille!

SECTION 1
FOUNDATIONS

1.

What Is Microlearning?

Chapter Questions

At the end of this chapter, you should be able to answer:

- What is microlearning?
- What is microlearning not?
- What are some examples of effective microlearning?
- What are the advantages of microlearning?

Is microlearning a text message? Is it a video? Does it need to be shorter than five minutes? Is it just "chunking" a course into smaller pieces? Is it bigger than a breadbox? Is it larger than a molecule?

Many questions swirl around the term *microlearning,* and until recently, there were few answers. Or, more precisely, few answers could be found in one place. Here we attempt to converge all the definitions, research, practice, and implementation of microlearning into a single guidebook, providing a road map for you to visualize, create, and deploy the microlearning you need. We're offering the short and sweet of microlearning.

Microlearning in Action

Let's start with examples of the concept of microlearning. Perhaps you already have a definition. As you read the following scenarios, see if your definition aligns with them (and know that it might not fit all instances). If you don't already have a preferred definition, be prepared to glean a lot of what microlearning is, because the idea has many layers.

Persuading Healthier Living Habits

Diabetes is a serious illness. Fortunately, in many pre-diabetic individuals, type 2 diabetes can be prevented by lifestyle modifications, such as additional exercise and cutting down on sugary foods and beverages. To that point, researchers studied the effects of microlearning's ability to alter the lifestyles of Indian men with impaired glucose tolerance.

The participants were randomly assigned to either a control group or a mobile phone messaging program. The test group received two text messages a day encouraging them to eat right and exercise. The control group received a standard one-time training and education program, during which they received information about eating correctly and the value of a modified lifestyle to prevent the onset of type 2 diabetes.

After two years, the cumulative incidence of diabetes was lower in those who received text messages than in the control group. The results were statistically significant. In fact, the microlearning presented to the men twice daily resulted in a relative risk reduction of 36 percent (Ramachandran et. al 2013).

Increasing Employee Engagement and Having Fun

Intercontinental Hotels Group (IHG) is a global company including nine hotel brands in nearly 100 countries. Their vision is to become one of the great companies in the world by creating "great hotels guests love." The company values its people and believes quality is important. So, it wanted to explore innovation in the area of training for existing members of the quality team. It also wanted to improve on the consistency and knowledge base of its employees.

IHG decided to use a gamified platform called mLevel that would provide "missions," or microlearning modules delivered with traditional game elements such as points and leaderboards but also with a game interface. Employees could play games and learn about quality.

The team selected for training was located in North America and Latin America; each team member (called a quality consultant) is responsible for maintaining quality standards at the up to 60–70 IHG hotel properties they each serve. The team director had two goals for the program: to engage the quality consultants to participate in training and enjoy it, and to measure their knowledge attainment by assessing where they started out versus what they learned after completing the training program.

Results showed that the program worked in terms of motivating the team—when asked about their motivation to play, 64 percent of the team members wanted to increase their knowledge and skill of brand standards, and 29 percent were motivated by their love of competition and wanting to be the best. According to a survey of the team members, 100 percent of the participants were interested in using games and microlearning for future program and process roll-outs. Additionally, the participants would recommend the gamified solution to a colleague 9.2 times out of 10. In answering a survey question about whether they had fun playing and learning, the result was a score of 4.4 out of 5 (mLevel 2015).

Offering Post-Instruction Product Review

Juan has just watched the new product launch. He is overwhelmed by the amount of information that was presented during the hour-and-a-half webinar, and now he needs to memorize the features and functionality so he can begin selling it effectively. How is he going to do that when he was barely able to remember everything from last month's product launch?

Fortunately for Juan, his company has just implemented a new educational app to help with product launches. Every day for four weeks, Juan receives a message encouraging him to answer three multiple-choice questions about the new product launch. The questions are timed, so he has to be quick to answer; to make things even more intense, he is competing against other salespeople in the organization. He has to be fast and correct with his answers to climb up the leaderboard.

Juan is doing alright—he isn't at the top of the leaderboard, but he's not at the bottom either. What Juan likes best is that he's recalling the information and concepts from the questions every time he is on a sales call. He is learning the information almost effortlessly and is even having fun answering the questions. The app presents questions he answers incorrectly more frequently than those he gets right. He also has begun studying the company's website, so he can be prepared to answer upcoming questions. His next goal is to move up on the leaderboard.

But Juan isn't the only one noticing the usage or engagement with the app. In fact, his firm is noticing some dramatic advantages. For one, after the initial 90-minute webinar, the sales force was in the field selling, not sitting in a classroom or behind a computer learning about the new product.

Second, they noticed that compared with all the launches done in the two years before this one, the sales team built one of the quickest pipelines for this product ever. The approach of quizzing sales people with product information on a daily basis both improved product knowledge and helped the team build the sales pipeline quickly and effectively.

Prompting Recall of Procedures

Having only been on the job for two weeks, it was hard for Jane to remember every little detail about how to take a customer order. She had to remember how to check the credit score, how to look up the right product when the customer didn't know the product number, and how to properly save the order and open another when a new customer was on the line.

When it was time for her first return, she got nervous. She vaguely remembered something about customer returns from the training class, but she could not remember exactly what she needed to do; her palms were starting to get clammy. Fortunately, as she looked at the queue of incoming calls, she also saw the button next to the caller ID, which said, "Review Returns." When she clicked the button, a short, 15-second video appeared reminding her of the steps that she needed to take and what was required from the customer for a return.

After watching the video, she took the call from the customer. Within two minutes, she was able to handle the return, refund the customer's credit card, and move on to the next call.

Practicing for Academic Pay-Offs

Ashley was studying organic chemistry and ran into a road block. She was having major trouble recalling all the terms and definitions. She couldn't remember the difference between *dissociation* and *disproportionation*, not to mention the definition of *tautomerism* and a hundred other terms. She needed a methodology to wrap her head around all these terms and definitions. Luckily for her, she had three classes with the smartest first-year student, Nancy.

One day over lunch, Ashley asked Nancy how she had memorized all those organic chemistry terms. Nancy said that she had downloaded a flash card app and entered every term and corresponding definition from the textbook into the app. Now, she quizzes herself daily on the terms, taking advantage of the app's ability to track which definitions she gets right and which she gets wrong.

Flashcards? Ashley was a little skeptical. She thought that was an elementary school trick, not something for a serious topic like organic chemistry. Nancy disagreed—she knew a lot of chem and bio majors who used flash card apps, and even had friends in medical school who used them.

Ashely decided to give the app a try and was amazed at how much better she performed on her next organic chemistry test. She now uses digital flash cards for every class, and is well on her way to making the Dean's list for the first time ever.

So, are these the types of examples that come to mind when you think about microlearning? Have they expanded your idea of the concept? Have they narrowed it?

Our examples show the potential we have to change behaviors, increase knowledge, and hone skills in mere minutes every day. We can do this by creating quick, meaningful interactions through games, quizzes, flashcards, videos, and text messages. We can push microlearning to learners or, as learners, we can pull microlearning to help ourselves. In summary, microlearning relies on a goal or objective, interactions, and the delivery mechanism for its success. We'll dig into these attributes next by defining *microlearning*.

What Is Microlearning?

It turns out that defining microlearning is not as simple as you might think. The current reality of microlearning is that it's constantly evolving and changing. Vendors, educational institutions, and training departments are working hard to implement a somewhat nebulous and elusive concept. But when it comes to microlearning in general, many professionals ask, "What exactly is it?"

Many have defined the concept of microlearning. Here are a few:

- Carla Torgerson, a pioneer in the microlearning space and author of *The Microlearning Guide to Microlearning*, defines it as "A piece of learning content that can be consumed in no more than five minutes" (Torgerson 2016).
- Shannon Tipton, a knowledgeable and well-known expert in microlearning, provides this insight: "Your microlearning creation will need to address the desire of people to learn any time in any place, placing people in control of their learning destiny. Microlearning is simple, short, and engaging. This is not to say we are 'dumbing down' learning for the sake of being short or narrow focused. Quite the opposite. When appropriately applied, microlearning can allow for deeper encoding, reflection, and practice retrieval—all necessary for the successful exchange of knowledge and learning application" (Tipton 2017).
- Author Theo Hug offers a slightly more academic take on microlearning. In his chapter in *Didactics of Microlearning*,

Helmwart Hierdeis sums up Hug's definition of microlearning as "an expression of a specific perspective which, in contrast to meso and macro aspects, is directed towards relatively small and time-restricted learning units and activities." Hug primarily defines microlearning as not being meso, which is an intermediate level of learning design (course level), or macro, which is at the global or overall curriculum level. It's the smallest instructional unit (Hierdeis 2007).

- JD Dillon, chief learning architect at the microlearning platform company Axonify, has been working with microlearning for more than 10 years. He uses the following to define microlearning: "Microlearning is an approach to training that delivers content in short, focused bites. To be effective, microlearning must fit naturally into the daily workflow, engage employees in voluntary participation, be based in brain science (how people actually learn), adapt continually to ingrain the knowledge employees need to be successful, and ultimately drive behaviors that impact specific business results" (Dillon 2018).

- Learning expert Will Thalheimer describes microlearning as "relatively short engagements in learning-related activities— typically ranging from a few seconds up to 20 minutes (or up to an hour in some cases)—that may provide any combination of content presentation, review, practice, reflection, behavioral prompting, performance support, goal reminding, persuasive messaging, task assignments, social interaction, diagnosis, coaching, management interaction, or other learning-related methodologies" (Thalheimer 2017).

After gleaning insights from these statements and definitions and clarifying our own thoughts on the subject, we will use the following definition for the purposes of this book:

> Microlearning is an instructional unit that provides a short engagement in an activity intentionally designed to elicit a specific outcome from the participant.

Let's look at each element of the definition:

- **Instructional unit.** An instructional unit is a start-to-finish learning or performance-enabling experience. Everything the participant needs is contained within the unit. It can be a learning activity, a video, a text message, work instructions, a performance prompt, or a flash card. One entire piece of instruction provides all the elements necessary to achieve the desired outcome. In other words, it stands by itself.

- **Short engagement.** In microlearning, the experience is not meant to last beyond a few minutes. The exact number of minutes is not universally agreed upon. We've seen the time-frame for microlearning defined as a few seconds or as long as an hour. So, a one-size-fits-all time constraint doesn't work. Naturally, different learning or performance needs require different lengths of time. The goal of the microlearning experience should be focused on achieving a singular outcome, without any fluff or extraneous information. In keeping it concentrated, microlearning is kept brief.

- **Engagement.** Without some type of engagement or a method to hold the participant's attention, the value of microlearning is lost. Engagement occurs when the participant's attention is tuned into the microlearning event and they voluntarily agree to take part in the microlearning. Engagement can take the form of gamification (forced engagement), a buzzing or beeping emitted from an educational app (sensory engagement), or the participant's desire to "need to know" during the flow of their work (self-prompted engagement).

- **Activity.** Passively watching a video or absent-mindedly reading a message does not create an activity or lead to a desired outcome. The learning or performance improvement portion of microlearning is a direct result of some type of action or activity being evoked. Research is clear that most knowledge gains occur when a person is involved in an activity to reinforce the learning. The activity might be as subtle as a mental activity, "consider three options for solving this problem," or as overt as a physical activity, "take the wrench and twist the bolt in a clockwise direction to tighten."

- **Intentionally designed.** Haphazardly chopping up an hourlong course into five-minute pieces and calling it microlearning will not produce the learning outcomes you intend. The process of designing microlearning must be intentional or the desired outcome may not be achieved. Too much money and time goes into education and corporate training to allow learning to occur by happenstance.

- **Elicit a specific outcome.** One of the first things that should be considered when designing microlearning is to determine what the outcome of the microlearning should be—for example, to pass a test, properly assemble an item, or act or behave in a certain way. The product's design should then help to facilitate that specific outcome, which would be less likely to occur without the learning program. This will focus the design and provide a measurable result.

- **Participant.** Notice we've purposefully avoided the terms *learner* and *student*. We think the term *participant* best captures the fact that the person participating in the microlearning event may successfully assemble a bicycle when the event is completed, but may not have stored the exact steps to do so in long-term memory. In essence, microlearning is not just about learning. In fact, many instances of microlearning are focused on performance—what the participant is going to do as a result of the microlearning experience.

When put together, these elements suggest an engaging but brief experience to achieve a focused outcome. Microlearning's true intent goes beyond a timeframe and beyond content, which many definitions emphasize.

Now that we know what microlearning is, let's discuss what it is not.

What Microlearning Is Not

Not every learning approach works effectively under every circumstance—there is no one-size-fits-all learning solution. The same can be said about microlearning. To that point, microlearning is not:

- **New.** Despite the rapid growth in interest for microlearning, it has been in use for a long time. If you look at microlearning from the perspective of performance support, Gloria Gery wrote about it in 1991 in her groundbreaking book, *Electronic Performance Support Systems*. If you count flash cards as a form of microlearning, it goes back to the 1800s or 1900s. And if you think about it, people likely shared small, critical pieces of information with one another before the advent of written language to convey knowledge about safety, appropriate foods to eat, and where to find water. Even the term *sharable content object* (SCO), which was part of the SCORM effort, represented the smallest possible instructional unit. Microlearning is not a new concept; its application has simply grown with the advent of mobile technology.

- **A complete learning ecosystem.** Microlearning should not be viewed as a replacement for other types of learning delivery, including classroom instruction, e-learning modules, games, and simulations. Rather, it is part of a larger learning ecosystem. Microlearning should be used in conjunction with other delivery methods to ensure the participant's journey toward mastery or the desired behavior is a success. It is not possible to expect one single method to meet every instructional need. Microlearning is not a panacea.

- **A resource library.** While resource libraries have their own value, they are not microlearning. The emphasis should be on some sort of learning or performance outcome because of the microlearning experience. Simply looking up a definition isn't microlearning. For example, if a person goes to SharePoint and downloads their organization's style guide and standard PowerPoint slide deck for internal presentations, they are using resources as resources, not as a microlearning event. Yes, the individual may have learned something from the application of the standards and the slide deck, but the materials were not designed to be educational; they were created to ensure consistency and reduce time in production. Additionally, the resource library did not provide expectations of what to present or teach the user how to create a presentation flow. If we continue to examine this example, we will see that the resource library, in many ways, serves one function, whereas learning serves a larger purpose.

- **Right for every learning outcome.** Chesley "Sully" Sullenberger could not have landed his distressed Airbus A320-214 in the freezing cold Hudson River safely if all his aviation experience was based on microlearning. He needed the deep learning that came from practicing with a glider, hours spent in a flight simulator, and his experience as a flight instructor. Microlearning cannot help you "connect the dots" like other forms of learning; it's not meant for deep reflection or building expertise or systems knowledge or complex problem solving. Skill development takes time and experience through contextual application, which microlearning is not designed to do. Our earlier example of Juan may make you say, "But Juan used microlearning to sell better." However, Juan was not being taught selling techniques; he was using microlearning to gain more information about the features and functions of the new product. Yes, microlearning assisted in his ability to sell the product, but there are also skills involved in selling, such as handling objections or assessing the body language and tone of the potential buyer, that were not part of the microlearning activities Juan used. This is a deeper level of learning that microlearning is not meant to accomplish.

- **Shrunken head learning.** Forcing someone to go through a microlearning course originally designed for a longer, more in-depth format is a recipe for disaster. For example, you can't simply chop up a one-hour course into five-minute increments and then shrink the training interface down to fit onto a smartphone. When you do this, all the outcomes of the one-hour course are still in place, whereas a true piece of microlearning would have only one outcome per activity or event. Creating an effective microlearning experience is a significant undertaking. A great deal of upfront planning to determine the right design and delivery for the microlearning experience is necessary for optimal success.

- **About knowledge.** When you focus on performance and behavior change to design microlearning (and most types of learning), the outcomes will be far more effective than if you merely focus on content or knowledge acquisition. When designing microlearning, you need to decide what you want the participant to do, not what they need to know.

- **Wholesale replacement for other learning initiatives.**
The results of microlearning are not about the creation of expertise or deep connections. The results are quick and context-based, centered on a performance or behavior need. This means we cannot abandon two-day or week-long leadership seminars or forgo the weeks of study involved in a college course. Microlearning is good for declarative and conceptual knowledge, but not as good for problem-solving or life and death situations that require a high level of depth and expertise. It's also not suitable for building deep expertise in

a subject area. The learner, to build mastery, needs to create mental models of how to approach a problem or a situation, and that is not the goal of microlearning.

Did your understanding of microlearning encompass any of these "are nots"? Perhaps these perspectives have refined your view of how to use microlearning effectively.

Now that we've outlined the what microlearning is and what microlearning is not, we can see that microlearning is simply another resource in our talent and learning development toolkit. No instructional delivery method can replace all other methods, and microlearning is no exception.

Keeping this new understanding of microlearning in mind, let's look at two other key discussion points related to the use of it.

Integration and Formality

Rarely does any single learning event or methodology exist in isolation. As we stated previously, microlearning is not meant to replace a whole learning system; it is meant to be used as part of one. You'll typically find it integrated at the lowest level of learning, created by a learning development specialist or informally developed by users as they learn.

Recall the definition ascribed to Theo Hug, which described the macro, meso, and micro levels of learning. Macrolearning is seen as the larger topic being mastered—for example, a degree in chemistry. Meso is more of an intermediate unit, such as an Organic Chemistry 101 course. Mesolearning could also relate to the lessons within a course, because those also represent mid-level learning in context to the class itself. If you are comfortable with our working definition of microlearning, then you know that it fits in last, as the smallest unit of instruction possible.

Using one of our prior examples, a student taking organic chemistry may use a flashcard app, a form of microlearning, to remember terminology. This represents an informal integration of microlearning. A faculty member may also include microlearning as part of the formal course structure. Let's say to assist students in testing their ability to do multi-step organic synthesis, the class has a quiz-styled activity that presents several different reaction sequences. The students are then prompted to determine the major product for each one. Students can engage in this activity as much as they want. Even if the class does not have an online component, the same activity could be done using a worksheet requiring students to show the reaction sequences for the synthesis of different molecules.

The main difference between formal and informal microlearning is that formal microlearning is integrated into the meso and macro structures of the learning, whereas when the participant informally creates their own microlearning it's likely based on self-motivation to learn or master something. You'll see informal learning, whether microlearning or not, in corporate, government, nonprofit, and educational organizations. The question for these institutions is how and where, if at all, formal microlearning supports the larger organizational learning ecosystem. Although this may not seem possible, if we think about the macro, meso, and micro levels of learning, we know that good instructional design aligns the outcomes of the smallest unit of instruction up the learning hierarchy.

In our educational example, the student's informal use of the flashcard app was to aid in recalling definitions. This could be mapped back to either a lesson or course outcome, depending on whether the student used the app to input all definitions as they are presented in lesson or if the student simply used the app for a specific lesson that was extremely difficult.

In the corporate world, the macro level represents the strategic outcomes of the organization, the *meso* represents the departmental outcomes aligned to the overall organizational outcomes, and the *micro* represents the team's or individual employee's outcomes that map back to the departmental outcomes. Each of these levels of outcomes supports the overall goal.

Short and Sweet

With an understanding of our definition of microlearning, and how the micro aspect feeds into the macro and meso aspects of learning, you can see how microlearning can happen organically or formally, as long as the smallest unit of instruction is mapped back to higher outcomes. As we will show throughout the book, the best uses of microlearning are when it is integrated into a larger learning design.

How do we know this? Well, research of course! We know doing research isn't everyone's favorite thing, so we did the leg work for you. Chapter 2 highlights significant research that supports the benefits of using microlearning and how it can affect performance-based outcomes. We also tie this research to the six use cases for microlearning that we outline. This will help you begin connecting the benefits of microlearning to the type of performance outcome you seek for your learners.

Key Takeaways

The following considerations will help you demystify what microlearning is:

- Microlearning has been around for a while. It's not a new idea or concept.
- Microlearning is a short, focused learning event, but is not based on an arbitrary time limit. Time should not be the defining element of microlearning.
- Microlearning needs to be part of a larger learning structure or strategy to optimize its effectiveness. When it stands by itself, each microlearning product only has a singular outcome. Therefore, it cannot provide an opportunity for wholistic mastery of any topic.
- Although microlearning it is mostly used for performance measures, it can be utilized for general knowledge recall.
- Microlearning should be engaging and encourage participation from the user during the learning event. Action and activity should be design elements of a microlearning event.
- Microlearning is not always the best solution, given how it is applied. Chopping up an existing course into smaller learning segments, creating a resource library, or mastering an advanced skill in totality are all common misuses and misperceptions of microlearning.

2.
Learning Principles and Microlearning

Chapter Questions

At the end of this chapter, you should be able to answer these questions:
- How can learning theory influence microlearning design?
- Which learning theories support microlearning design?
- Which learning domain am I trying to influence?

If microlearning is not new, why all the buzz right now? Thought leaders, vendors, and practitioners alike now tout microlearning as the must-have innovation to improve the efficacy of learning. Its popularity likely stems from recent technological innovations in mobile devices, as well as the increased access and experience digital natives have with the technology. Seriously! Robyn's friend's four-year-old can launch an app with two swift swipes and a tap on an iPad.

Many articles treat microlearning as if it were the be-all-to-end-all, if you will. But is it really a panacea for learning and learners? Of course not! Microlearning is just another way to design learning materials, although it has a larger role today thanks to the current culture's growing desire for on-demand information.

This chapter focuses on the foundational aspects or principles that all sound learning should be designed upon: learning theories and domains. In our context, learning theories are paradigms that provide perspective on how people acquire, retain, and recall knowledge and learning, while learning domains represent classifications for how we attain knowledge, skills, and behaviors. Implementation is also an essential part of determining design, but we'll cover that in chapter 6.

Learning Theories

Like any other method of learning design, microlearning relies on applicable learning theory. There are three well-established perspectives on how one learns: behaviorism, cognitivism, and constructivism. A fourth, connectivism, discusses how the learner connects or "plugs in" to acquire knowledge. Each theory represents an opportunity to use microlearning, but also supports principles for how to design it. Let's start with behaviorism.

Behaviorism

Perhaps one of the most well-known examples of behaviorism is the case of Pavlov's dogs. Pavlov conducted studies where he conditioned dogs to associate a bell ringing with food. But Pavlov was not alone; other researchers have conducted similar experiments to attempt to determine how learning worked. For example, B.F. Skinner conditioned lab rats to push a lever to be rewarded with food. Pavlov's approach is considered classical conditioning, where learning is associated with an event or stimulus. Skinner's approach is operant conditioning, which suggests behaviors have associated consequences, both good and bad. He conducted research examining how changes in behavior influence how we retain knowledge.

One element of behaviorism is that the researchers tend to focus on the learner as a passive recipient of information. Thus the underlying concept is that learners acquire knowledge through negative or positive reinforcement. As an example, did you ever show up to class late only to find your teacher had locked the door? This would probably only have to happen once to guarantee that from that time forward you showed up before the door was locked. This is an example of behaviorism at play. Your behavior: arriving late. Negative reinforcement: being locked out. Change in behavior: arriving on time.

So, how does behaviorism support microlearning? In the 1950s, Skinner introduced teaching machines, or programmed instruction, which became one of his most important influences on the tenets of instructional design. In fact, Skinner's programmed instruction format is evident in microlearning through:

- content being presented in small, soundly designed segments
- learner interactions with the content
- feedback provided to the learner through their interactions
- learner control over the pace of the content.

Let's return to the example of Ashley and her flashcard app in chapter 1. Ashley would know immediately if she had the correct response once the app provided the definition for the term. Additionally, she could go through as many or as few terms as she wanted, at her own pace.

Cognitivism

Cognitivism takes us away from the passive learner in behaviorism to a learner attempting to make meaning through association or observation (or both). Under this learning theory, the stimulus does not condition the learner to acquire new information. Instead, the learner processes information and determines how they will store that information for later recall.

One active researcher and theorist in the area of cognitivism is Albert Bandura, who did extensive work in observational learning. In his experiments using Bobo dolls (those inflatable dolls where the bottom is rounded so it cannot fall over), he demonstrated that children learn through imitation. If a child observed an adult attacking the Bobo doll, the child would do the same (Bandura, Ross, and Ross 1961). Bandura later conceptualized social cognitive theory (SCT), which contends that the personal factors of the learner, the learner's behavior, and their environment work together in a reciprocal network. This reciprocity influences how the learner encodes the information presented.

In some respects, cognitivism takes the approach of a learner's mind being much like a computer with the ability to input and output information. Computers are structured or programmed to store information and then release that information based on specific commands. A learner, in some sense, will do the same. The difference is that the learner's mind is not pre-programmed, so they're responsible for how they encode information for future recall.

So, how does cognitivism support microlearning? How do we help learners use more computer-like characteristics to make meaning? The following techniques illustrate instructional design principles that also support effective microlearning creation:

- ordering and organizing information based on priority
- visually cuing information for value, relevance, or importance
- forming associations to prior experiences and knowledge
- grouping or chunking information into logical groupings

- using mnemonics or other techniques for information storage and retrieval.

Pulling again from chapter 1, let's think about the patients receiving messages and reminders as part of their diabetes care regimen. Although we are not privy to everything in the messages, we imagine that information was emphasized by how they styled the font—for example, bolding statistics to highlight positive or negative habits for diabetics. Another approach may have been to have the patient recall simple, fun activities they did as children, such as riding a bike or taking a walk in the woods. This association to former information may influence the patient to see healthy activities not so much as new hurdles to master, but as things they already know and can do.

The messages may have also been grouped to focus on core habits that improve a diabetic's overall quality of life. The first grouping could focus on general diabetic self-management, the second could zero in on dietary habits, the third message group could focus on exercise, and so on.

Going further, they could share a mnemonic to ease the retrieval of information. For instance, "GLUCOSE BAD" introduces the overall concept of diabetic self-management for the whole body (Glycemic control, Lipids, Urine screening, Cigarettes, Ophthalmic exams, Sexual dysfunction, Extremities, Blood pressure, Aspirin, and Dental exams). These 10 items are all elements of controlling diabetes. Some are to be avoided and some are to be implemented on a regular basis. The mnemonic helps a person keep diabetes management essentials top-of-mind. Then they could follow each statement in the mnemonic with a definition, an explanation of its relevance to diabetic self-management, and some techniques to assist in its management.

Constructivism

Constructivism focuses on how learners continuously attempt to make meaning based on their experiences, conduct, and the environment around them. As with cognitivism, constructivism asserts that learners engage in their surroundings and dynamically build comprehension through social and cognitive processes. Or in simple terms, they interact with the environment and the people within it.

Constructivism as we know it today is a blend of the theories of John Dewey (not to be confused with Melvil Dewey, the inventor of the Dewey Decimal System), Jean Piaget, and Lev Vygotsky. Dewey believed that learning should be contextualized or "real world" and that learners should have an opportunity to demonstrate their knowledge. Piaget postulated that learners construct knowledge by testing what they know; he also believed that this knowledge acquisition occurs regardless of social context.

Vygotsky, on the other hand, asserted that the social construct can and does have an effect on the learner, which then founded his theory of social constructivism. Vygotsky's most popular work, the Zone of Proximal Development, posits that learners can acquire knowledge through means of collaborating with peers or educators (Gredler 1997).

Consider a teenager learning to drive in a simulator that mimics a car's control and handling in different environmental and road conditions. This is a constructivist way of learning. Likewise, putting the teen in a real car on real roads with a driving instructor would also be constructivism at play.

So, how does constructivism support microlearning? You might place a learner in a context that emulates the situation they need to resolve with the resources they need to create a solution. Through the learner's interactions they develop meaning, understanding, and eventually (hopefully) an answer to the presented problem. Along the way, the learner should discover an approach to solve the problem and what information was most valuable in the situation to resolve it.

A good real-world example would be a pharmaceutical sales representative who wants to leave materials about different drugs at a physician's office. The representative would need the skills to artfully handle any of the doctor's objections to the material in the pursuit of gaining support for use of the drug. More than likely the sales rep will log several hours of role playing during their initial training, be coached by a sales trainer or regional manager, and then practice on their own to finesse responses.

A microlearning opportunity here could be a short video that covers a specific objection. The sales representative could play the first part of the video to learn the objection, pause the video, script their response, and then return to the video to play out the method in which the actor handled the objection. The sales rep would then compare their scripted response to how the actor handled it, to determine how well they did.

Connectivism

Connectivism is the integration of principles explored by chaos, network, complexity, and self-organization theories as defined by George Siemens and Stephen Downes (Siemens 2005; Downes 2010). Connectivism embraces the use of technology and the desire to make connections for meaning and learning, focusing on managing knowledge and gaining comprehension at the time of need. However, learning may be misguided if the learner is not adept at tying together the information they connected. Furthermore, the learner may not comprehend that while the connection is right for the current situation, it may be completely wrong for another. Their learning can also be skewed if the connections they made were to items with inaccuracies or errors.

Connectivism focuses on the here and now, and developing skills to find what the learner needs as opposed to focusing on what the learner already knows. As Siemens (2005) states: "The pipe is more important than the content within the pipe." With the evolution of knowledge at the ready, access to accurate, reliable information at the time of need, and the comprehension of how to access and use it will become more important than what the learner currently knows.

The principles of connectivism are as follows (Siemens 2005):

- Learning and knowledge rests in a diversity of opinions.
- Learning is a process of connecting specialized nodes or information sources.
- Learning may reside in nonhuman appliances.
- The capacity to know more is more critical than what is currently known.
- Nurturing and maintaining connections are needed to facilitate continual learning.
- Ability to see connections between fields, ideas, and concepts is a core skill.
- Currency (accurate, up-to-date knowledge) is the intent of all connectivist learning activities.
- Decision-making is itself a learning process. Choosing what to learn and the meaning of incoming information is seen through the lens of a shifting reality. While there is a right answer now, it may be wrong tomorrow due to alterations in the information climate affecting the decision.

So, how can connectivism support microlearning? Let's return to the idea of knowledge management. In chapter 1 we were introduced to Jane and her need to recall the process for returns. The "how to" for returns was connected directly to the customer on hold, allowing Jane to review the steps for returns prior to handling the call.

● ● ●

Learning theories tell us how people learn. You will take this into consideration for any learning program you choose to design. However, theories are not used alone in formulating sound instructional materials. It is also necessary to understand the learning content and the complexity of it when creating instruction. This includes the classification of content and skills—the "what people learn"—which is also known as a learning domain.

Learning Domain

When examining microlearning, it's important to consider the learning domain you are attempting to influence. You might want an employee to learn the features and functionality of a product, or a student to learn the names of countries around the world. You might be instructing employees to appreciate the importance of acting in a safe and compliant manner, or you might be teaching art appreciation. You might want someone to learn how to change a part on a piece of equipment, or how to use a pipet properly.

Each of these different types of learning outcomes tap a different learning domain. Making a conscious decision about what learning domain the microlearning product will affect helps you construct the microlearning and align the design with the desired learning outcome.

In this section, we will discuss the three major learning domains to consider: cognitive, affective, and psychomotor.

Cognitive Domain

Where would organizations be without knowledgeable, competent employees who can think on their feet by recalling and performing the functions of their job? The cognitive domain centers on two aspects: knowledge and comprehension. It is what we most often think about when we mention the word *learning*. From run-of-the-mill HR policies to very defined processes specific to a position, the cognitive domain is at the root of almost all work. Microlearning can work with cognitive-based content in multiple ways to keep employees up to date without disrupting their daily workflow.

In the cognitive domain, learners progress from simpler functions like reciting or recognizing information to more complex functions like analyzing or evaluating a situation based on the information they know. For example, memorizing the names of a piece of equipment's parts is a cognitive skill, as is troubleshooting that same piece of equipment using logical deduction and a problem-solving protocol.

This concept of cognitive growth is represented with Benjamin Bloom's Taxonomy, which was published in the mid-1950s and updated in the early 2000s by Lorin Anderson and David Krathwohl. Bloom's Taxonomy arranges the acquisition and application of knowledge from low-level processing to higher-order thinking skills. The terminology of each version of the taxonomy is listed in Table 2-1.

Additionally, Table 2-1 indicates which levels of knowledge are most appropriate for microlearning and which learning theories we see as complementary to each classification. You will notice that the three lowest levels of Bloom's Taxonomy—knowledge/remember, comprehension/understanding, and application/applying—are the most appropriate for microlearning.

Table 2-1. Cognitive Domain Taxonomy

Bloom's Term	Anderson and Krathwohl's Term	Combined Definition	Appropriate for Microlearning	Associated Learning Theory
Knowledge	Remembering	Demonstrate memorization of previously learned material. Focused on recall.	Yes	Behaviorism
Comprehension	Understanding	Organize ideas, compare and contrast concepts, and summarize content and ideas.	Yes	Behaviorism
Application	Applying	Apply previously learned knowledge to a situation.	Yes	Cognitivism
Analysis	Analyzing	Examine and break information into smaller parts and determine relationships to make inferences.	No	Cognitivism Constructivism Connectivism
Synthesis	Evaluating	Make a judgement related to a course of action or a set of criteria.	No	Constructivism
Evaluation	Creating	Combine elements together in a new pattern; create something original.	No	Constructivism Connectivism

When you get to the higher-level thinking skills, other forms of learning are more effective. It takes a great deal of time and concentrated effort to be able to perform the mental processing required by analytics/

analyzing, synthesis/evaluation, and evaluation/creating. These thinking processes are appropriate for classroom instruction, workshops, mentoring, and apprenticeships, not standalone microlearning. It is hard to learn to create something like a business proposal from a series of microlearning snippets. However, it is possible to use microlearning to remind a person about the elements of the proposal.

So, how does teaching knowledge, comprehension, and application via microlearning play out as a solution that is less intrusive to an employee's workflow, but is also better for performance? Let's look at an increasingly necessary annual compliance subject: active shooter instruction. It's a sad reality faced by many organizations. Employees are usually brought together for a half-day or whole-day training experience, complete with classroom lecture, demonstration, and possibly simulation. At some point during the year, it's likely a surprise drill will be performed to assess preparedness and ability to minimize or stop the threat. Some organizations may also provide a self-paced course to review the subject and any valuable procedures and techniques being advocated to minimize threat.

Is learning how to handle an active shooter situation once a year an effective way to ensure all employees are mentally prepared to deal with this high-stress situation? Will an annual unplanned drill keep folks vigilant and prepared to use the skills and techniques they were taught? Perhaps, but wouldn't you rather be more confident?

Let's look at how you might use microlearning as a training solution: Using a series of communications, HR creates a microlearning campaign for staying safe and vigilant on campus. Each month is focused on a technique or skill to help reinforce the key takeaways from the standard one-day workshop. For example:

- April: Video-based message demonstrating how to barricade a door with a desk or table.
- May: A "what would you do" scenario, asking what your responsibility is if you see something suspicious outside your classroom window.
- June: A call-to-action in the form of a printable worksheet you use to inventory the building's exits and any items in your room or office that would make good barricades or weapons.

You can still follow the annual one-day training format and use the microlearning augment it, or you can use the microlearning as the annual training, just spread out over the entire year as opposed to pulling everyone together for it on one day. But what about new employees who have never had any training? What happens if a situation occurs and they've only been exposed to two months' worth of microlearning courses? Again, we didn't say throw the baby out with the bathwater! An annual workshop or a self-paced comprehensive program may be ideal. However, the point here is that you are expecting a lot from your learners if you think they're going to be able to recall critical, life-saving information during a high-stress situation from training they could have received more than 100 days ago. As you'll learn in the next chapter, microlearning can boost recall to improve performance.

That's the cognitive domain. But what about the self-efficacy of learners that is a driving force to performance, as we covered under Bandura and social cognitivism? What domain discusses behavior? The affective.

Affective Domain

Attitude and morale play a large part within any organization. While most of the time learning and development professionals don't think of their job as helping to teach attitudes, organizations engage in that practice all the time. The affective domain is the one that deals with emotions, attitudes, and values. Organizations like the United Way or Habitat for Humanity teach attitudes toward helping other people who are not as fortunate. Many companies run quality campaigns to teach a positive attitude toward quality initiatives or try to influence employees to adopt corporate values. Microlearning can be an effective tool in helping to shape attitudes within an organization.

In the affective domain, you want to try to move a person from ignoring an idea or concept to having them value the idea or concept and even, eventually, having them become a champion of the attitude you are trying to foster within the organization. Table 2-2 outlines several classifications for the affective domain, based on work done by David Krathwohl.

Table 2-2. Affective Domain Taxonomy

Krathwohl's Term	Definition	Appropriate Use of Microlearning	Associated Learning Theory
Receiving	Being aware of or attending to something in the environment.	Yes	Behaviorism
Responding	Exhibiting some new behavior as a result of an experience or learning.	Yes	Behaviorism Cognitivism
Valuing	Showing some definitive involvement or commitment and being willing to be perceived by others as valuing certain ideas, materials, or phenomena.	Yes	Cognitivism (Social) Connectivism
Organization	Integrating the new value or attitude into ones' general set of values.	Yes	Cognitivism Connectivism
Championing	Believing in something so strongly that the person becomes an active champion of the value and acts consistently in accordance with that value.	No	Cognitivism (Social) Contructivism Connectivism

As you can see from the progression, microlearning can be used to help learners receive and respond to values that you want them to adopt. However, moving to the highest level in the taxonomy typically requires methods other than microlearning to provide a lasting impact. The aspects of receiving, responding, valuing, and organization can be aligned to elements within social cognitivism and connectivism, whereas Championing embodies aspects of social cognitive theory, in addition to social constructivism and connectivism.

Teaching and influencing attitudes can be accomplished using several instructional strategies. These include an endorsement of the concept by a credible role model, testimonials, emotionally charged messages, or a sense of fun and well-being associated with the attitude.

One method frequently used by advertising agencies that can be easily copied by training and development is the use of a celebrity endorsement. Whether people admit it or not, they are influenced by celebrities or people who have achieved a great deal of success and whom they admire. To use this concept to your advantage, leverage people within the organization who are well known and well-respected to deliver the message through microlearning.

Your "celebrity" can be a well-known external consultant in the field related to quality or safety or even change management, or it can be an internal leader. It doesn't have to be the CEO of the organization, but short messages related to a specific topic have been found to be extremely powerful when delivered by a senior leader. They usually command a great deal of respect and if the technique is not overused, it does help influence others.

Another method is to use testimonials. Of course, it depends on your topic, but a message related to the importance of safety or change management from a frontline employee can help influence others. In a college or university setting, for example, you can have a recent alumnus talk about the importance of a course and how the content covered helped them with their first job after graduation.

A video testimonial provided in a microlearning format can be highly influential. If you've ever laughed, cried, or got angry at a commercial then you know that even 30 seconds of information can be emotionally charged. Constructing a message about the values of the company and tying it to the well-being of others or the community can help to reinforce company values and attitudes. One element in many of these pieces is the use of music to set the mood and tone. Music has a deep impact on our attitudes and can be used to influence how we are thinking and to associate certain images or ideas with a feeling.

When confronted with the tasks of influencing attitudes around change management, following new company policies, interacting with customers, deciding to enjoy or embrace an academic subject, or encouraging everyone to act in a safe, responsible manner, microlearning can play a key role. Providing short, targeted content related to influencing attitudes can be an effective way to use microlearning to achieve your desired outcomes.

Psychomotor Domain

Although not all our intelligent, motivated employees need to physically demonstrate competency in skills every day, we do know that motor skills are necessary for most work to be done successfully. This is what the psychomotor domain focuses on—the linkage between physical activities, motor skills, and mental processing. If you've ever watched a video on YouTube to help you change a faucet or a filter in your car, then you've used microlearning within the psychomotor domain. The goal of this type of microlearning is simply to perform a specific task that involves thinking and physical activity.

The psychomotor domain, like the cognitive and affective domains, has a hierarchy of skills ranging from the basic skill of perception to skilled movements and beyond. These were proposed by RH Dave in the 1970s. Table 2-3 shows how the foundational theories for Imitation and Manipulation are a blend of social constructivism and connectivism, whereas precision, articulation, and naturalization involve constructivism at play.

Table 2-3. Psychomotor Domain Taxonomy

Dave's Term	Definition	Appropriate Use of Microlearning	Associated Learning Theory
Imitation	Observing and copying someone else. Most likely a video or animation of a physical process.	Yes	Cognitivism (Social) Connectivism
Manipulation	Attempting the physical manipulation of tools and equipment guided via instruction to perform a skill.	Yes	Constructivism (Social) Connectivism
Precision	Demonstrating accuracy, proportion, and exactness in the skill performance without the presence of the original source.	No	Constructivism
Articulation	Combining, sequencing, and performing two or more skills consistently.	No	Constructivism
Naturalization	Combining, sequencing, and performing two or more skills consistently with ease, little physical or mental exertion, or automatically.	No	Constructivism

Let's take a look at another example where psychomotor skills play a critical performance role: a field technician. One task might be to change out the malfunctioning part of a piece of equipment. To do so, the technician will need to know how to diagnose the malfunction, identify the right part, disconnect the right part, choose the new part, and install it correctly. There is usually a procedure or a list of steps the individual must perform to successfully complete this task.

The steps can be outlined in the form of a poster, a video, or even written instruction. Video instructions containing an audio track explaining what the person is doing and how are especially beneficial. The individual viewing the instruction can pause or repeat sections of the video so they can adequately perform the task. However, the cost of developing audio and video instruction can deter these more thorough and contextual approaches. A quicker, more cost-effective method would be creating an animated GIF of each step. Both approaches embrace microlearning and both design approaches support it.

For microlearning in the psychomotor domain, the goal is typically not to have the person learn the skill or sequence of steps. Rather it is for the person to perform the sequence of steps at a high enough level to complete the task. Sometimes this is referred to as the "guided response" level of a psychomotor taxonomy, or the imitation level.

If the learner needs a higher level of proficiency in the psychomotor skill, you might consider other types of instruction that include prolonged and targeted practice. The microlearning could start with an overview of the process and then break it down into discreet steps, guiding the learner through each step. Make sure to show proper completion of each step and, if possible, methods the learner can use to check their progress.

When creating microlearning focused on the psychomotor domain, be sure to include images of properly positioned items and proper hand placement or other required physical movement. Use sensory cues to guide the learner's motor activity, such as an observation about the placement of a safety stop or the direction of a valve. Also include an explanation of how to transition from one movement to another so the learner understands the proper steps.

Short and Sweet

For any learning approach you choose, it's essential to build a base of knowledge and comprehension. In this chapter, we explained how microlearning embraces the traditional learning theories of behaviorism, cognitivism, and constructivism. We also discussed how it supports and perpetuates the theory of connectivism, especially when providing educational materials on social platforms such as YouTube or LinkedIn Learning.

Learning domains create a critical cross section with learning theories that highlight opportunities for using microlearning, especially when learning and development professionals have to determine the complexity (or domain classification) of the subject matter. Three factors—how we learn (theories), what we learn (domains), and why we learn (classification or taxonomy level)—help us select the appropriate use case for microlearning.

"What are use cases," you ask? In chapter 3, Uses of Microlearning, we'll introduce six use cases for microlearning. This will give you an opportunity to take your subject matter, which you've evaluated for the most appropriate learning theories and domains, and begin bringing your microlearning program to life!

Key Takeaways

Based on the information from this chapter, the following considerations will guide which principles and domains you apply to your microlearning:

- Microlearning design can be influenced by more than one learning theory.
- Microlearning can be used with each learning domain, but not all categories of each respective taxonomy are well suited for microlearning. For example, synthesis and evaluation are not ideal uses of microlearning in the cognitive domain.

3.

Uses of Microlearning

Chapter Questions

At the end of this chapter, you should be able to answer:

- What four ways can microlearning play a part in a larger training initiative?
- What are common uses for microlearning?
- What is the difference between a microlearning use case and a type of microlearning?
- What other considerations factor into determining the best use and type of microlearning?

What a build up to get to this chapter! First we clarified what microlearning is, and then we explained the theoretical principles and the classifications of each learning domain. Now it's time to discuss the uses of microlearning. We cover six uses, defining, contextualizing, and providing examples of each.

But before we get into each use case, let's make sure we're all on the same page in defining the difference between a use case for microlearning versus different types of microlearning.

A use case is determined by:

- theory—*how* we learn

- the domains of learning—*what type* of skill or information we will learn
- learning domain classification—*what level* of complexity of skill we want the learner to achieve.

The type of microlearning is the resulting product that was designed for the selected use case. The type of use case is determined more by factors of the project related to:

- the learner's preferences for learning
- the environment the learning will be delivered in
- the timeline for delivery
- the budget for the project.

Let's take a look at an example. Say you want to prepare learners for a larger learning event. As such, your selected use case will be preparatory (described below). You determine that your domain of learning is cognitive, and the classifications are knowledge and comprehension from Bloom's Taxonomy. Referring to Table 2-1 in chapter 2, you note that the selected classifications usually fall under the behaviorism learning theory. This means you could break down the learning into discrete pieces and provide reinforcement for correct and incorrect responses. From these insights, you can then choose any type of microlearning, from an infographic to a gamified app. The decision to use one type of microlearning over another relates to factors of type, not use.

Considerations for Use Cases

By now you are probably really thinking about your microlearning initiative. So, let's keep you thinking about it. How do you envision microlearning as part of the training initiative?

- Will it *supplement* the current training by offering different ways to engage the learner?
- Will it *reinforce* training content that is used often and is vital for job performance?
- Will it *augment* current learning materials and provide an opportunity to build confidence in performing tasks?
- Will it *remediate* poor or incorrect performance and behaviors?

With these four questions in mind, let's introduce the use cases.

Six Use Cases of Microlearning

The following six uses cases demonstrate opportunities for microlearning to play a part in your overall talent development strategy. We define and elaborate each use case with a work-related situation where the microlearning could provide further context to the explanation (and possibility) of use. The first column in Tables 3-1 to 3-6 is the use type. The second column highlights four design considerations. The third column provides a contextualized example. And the final column offers suggested measures to evaluate the performance. We recognize that evaluation of performance may not be done solely on the microlearning, so we offer ideas to evaluate it independently or to fold it into a larger evaluation plan.

Use Case 1. Pensive

When you present learners with pensive microlearning, you ask them to reflect upon an idea, situation, or learning task. The goal is to have the learner think through or brainstorm ideas or concepts using reflective inquiry. Pensive microlearning works well for augmenting and remediating.

Educational researcher and writer Roger Schank pioneered the underlying idea for digitized pensive microlearning. He developed a "sounding board" idea in his *Engines for Education* hyperbook, where he describes an automated process that walks the learner through a brainstorming session (Schank and Cleary 1995). Pensive microlearning's intent is to hone critical thinking and creative problem-solving. The goal is for the learner to formulate their own conclusions through the process of answering short, targeted questions. Schank envisioned the use of AI (artificial intelligence) and chat bot technology to provide the guiding interface for the learner, presenting a series of poignant questions to assist with the thinking process.

When you create a pensive microlearning program, you might ask questions that focus the user's attention on parts of the problem they may have been taking for granted, such as "What is my competitor doing in this area?" or "How are different industries dealing with this issue?" You might also design questions to help learners break through perceived constraints and eliminate barriers from consideration to highlight what the user really wants through questions such as, "If financial limitations were not an issue, what approach would you take to solving this problem?"

Even an inquiry that seems irrelevant can help. For instance, you might ask context-switching questions such as "What recreational activities are you good at?" or "Who is your favorite artist?" Context switching helps the learner forget about the problem at hand, which has been shown to lead to cognitive breakthroughs. Introducing a new subject or idea and then asking how the two issues relate may also spark a creative idea: "How would your favorite artist, Jackson Pollock, approach this problem?"

Table 3-1 demonstrates the use of pensive microlearning to assist project managers at Bee Naturals (BN) better contemplate risk when project planning. BN is a health and beauty company that uses raw honey as a key ingredient in all their products. The company wants to increase repeat sales of its signature line through improved marketing and sales tactics. It ultimately wants to reduce profit loss from unidentified or poorly managed risk within projects by 10 percent in the next quarter.

Table 3-1. Pensive-Based Microlearning Example

Use Case	Design Considerations	Contextualized Example	Possible Measures
Pensive	Learner	Project managers	• Compare project status prior to microlearning initiative with project status post initiative. • Track use of chat bot feature as part of project planning process and compare to outcomes of projects as related to risk versus a project that was planned without using the chat bot.
	Content	Company policies and processes on managing risk. General content on risk management.	
	Content Access	Chat bot mobile and web-based application	
	Development	Botsify, chat bot software	

Use Case 2. Performance

Performance-based microlearning represents just-in-time, point-of-need, or prompter support. You might provide performance microlearning as part of a workflow so the employee can complete a task with or without learning support. When you provide learning solutions at the time of need, the employee can reflect on the experience, rethink their performance, and reinforce the proper technique or correct an error. Performance microlearning can supplement, reinforce, and augment training.

In chapter 1, we wrote about the time Jane used a suggested 15-second video to help perform a return for a customer. A more intrusive version of this use case is pushing a prompt about performance to the user. This use can be designed to target specific areas of need or gaps in learner recall. Jane was not prompted to refresh herself on refunds; instead she chose to do that by selecting the Review Returns button. In contrast, if an employee enters information into an order entry system and forgets to check a customer's credit limit, the system might automatically prompt them to check the credit limit and then remind the employee of the importance and need to check the customer's credit limit every time.

The focus for performance microlearning is not on learning for the long term or even recalling knowledge; instead, it's on immediate or near-term performance. You may perform a task once (changing the showerhead in your shower) or you may perform it over and over again (tying a kayak onto your car's roof for transport). Other examples of performance microlearning include recalling the process to fill out a company mileage report, or reviewing the expectations for holding web-based conference calls prior to an online event.

Another instance would be how to write a constructive performance statement for a performance evaluation (as shown in Table 3-2). Here the managers at Bee Naturals need to write a statement to support a less-than-stellar performance rating. When completing the online performance evaluation form, the managers encounter a prompt to review writing constructive statements after providing the low score.

Table 3-2. Performance-Based Microlearning Example

Use Case	Design Considerations	Contextualized Example	Possible Measures
Performance	Learner	Managers	• Audit of evaluations from managers • Compare evaluations written before and after microlearning • Compare evaluations by that used e-learning to those who did not
	Content	Writing a constructive performance statement	
	Content Access	Organization portal through SharePoint	
	Development	E-learning module with video, including voice-over slides and an introduction from the VP of HR	

Use Case 3. Persuasive

Persuasive microlearning is meant to modify the behavior of the learner and is usually goal oriented. (You might also recall that this is linked to the affective domain.) In chapter 1 we shared the study on diabetic patients, which is an example of persuasive microlearning. The text messages participants received were designed to remind the patient to practice and incorporate healthier lifestyle choices and habits. The messages were sent every day in hopes that they would influence the learner to adopt some of the suggested habits and lifestyle modifications. Persuasive microlearning supports augmenting and remediating behavior.

Now let's look at how persuasive microlearning could be used to train the warehouse workers at Bee Naturals. They need to maintain a hazard-free work floor, and BN knows that the routine aspects of jobs can desensitize workers to their environment. The company can use persuasive microlearning to change the behavior of its employees to be more visually vigilant to their work environment. In Table 3-3 we see that the organization has chosen a paper-based option to deliver their motivational messages.

Table 3-3. Persuasive-Based Microlearning Example

Use Case	Design Considerations	Contextualized Example	Possible Measures
Persuasive	Learner	Warehouse shift workers	• Compare accident reports before and after posting infographics • Quiz employees' retention of content using a survey with several scenarios before and after posting the infographic
	Content	Maintaining a hazard-free work floor	
	Content Access	Print and poster	
	Development	Infographic	

Use Case 4. Post-Instruction

Post-instruction microlearning complements a larger training initiative that a learner has taken. This type of microlearning distills the key concepts from a larger training program into bite-sized pieces for use in refresher courses that are either scheduled by the organization or readily available to learners. Post-instruction microlearning can be supplemental, reinforcing, or augmenting.

This use case has plenty of options for incorporation. However, this also means that it's easy to overuse. Does every piece of training really need post-instruction follow-through? Is there a standard that the organization or a position within the organization must maintain because it is critical?

In Table 3-4, we look at how Bee Naturals is reconsidering its approach to the annual diversity and inclusion (D&I) training. BN believes that the diversity of its workforce is part of what sets it apart. While there isn't currently a D&I problem, the company wants to model an everyday philosophy on matters of diversity and inclusion. This approach will give more attention to the concepts and discussion points that traditionally get compressed during the annual D&I training.

Table 3-4. Post-Instruction-Based Microlearning Example

Use Case	Design Considerations	Contextualized Example	Possible Measures
Post-Instruction	Learner	All employees	• Survey of employee's comprehension of diversity and inclusion pre and post-instruction • Short quiz at the end of each staged initiative for use in comparison and retention • Compare incidents associated to diversity and inclusion pre- and post-implementation
	Content	Diversity and inclusion	
	Content Access	Staged communications with a link to content located on organization's HR webpage	
	Development	Varied use of contextualized videos and animations	

Use Case 5. Practice

Practice-based microlearning serves as both a reminder to practice and a coach to help hone a skill. Anders Ericsson's work in deliberate practice shows that improving a person's skills requires breaking a skill or behavior into small, achievable, well-defined steps (Ericsson and Pool 2016). Practice provides opportunities to augment, reinforce, or remediate training.

Consider an example we provide in the beginning of chapter 7 (you may want to take a look now). In the example, employees from NBCU receive a prompt to practice speaking into a presentation app every day. The app provides visual cues to coach consistency, such as keeping the pace, tone, and volume of the person's speech fluid. The microlearning (or more accurately the short prompts) encouraged them to practice a skill and routinely provided feedback. It was also fast—designed to take only a few minutes each day.

With the advent of mobile technologies and apps, instructional designers can leverage different tools to both remind learners that they should practice and to provide instructions, feedback, and a way to monitor a person's progress. These tools help the learner practice in small increments with targeted, specific feedback that's also provided in small increments.

Practice-based microlearning can be used with any of the learning domains. We point this out because practice can get boiled down to a physical task or a routine need, but behaviors also need practice. For example, BN wanted the topic of diversity and inclusion to be more than a once-a-year discussion—employees received microlearning prompts to practice and integrate the concepts of diversity and inclusion as part of their daily behavior on the job.

A routine part of reporting for BN auditors is writing a reason or rationale to support a decision they've made. However, it's something their new auditors struggle with. Table 3-5 outlines the company's practice-based microlearning initiative, which provides opportunities for entry-level auditors to practice this task and build their confidence without risk.

Table 3-5. Practice-Based Microlearning Example

Use Case	Design Considerations	Contextualized Example	Possible Measures
Practice-Based	Learner	Entry-level auditors	• Evaluation of reports by manager • Checklist employee uses to verify that their statements of reason conform to standards • Frequency of and the specific subjects that the manager pushes out to all entry-level auditors compared with the material and frequency its pushed to a specific entry-level auditor
	Content	Standards of reporting: How to state reasons for when an overall opinion cannot be expressed.	
	Content Access	Custom mobile and web-based app used by entry-level auditors; managers can also push specific content out to all or select entry-level auditors through app	
	Development	Interactive infographics of annotated statements	

Use Case 6. Preparatory

Preparatory microlearning provides an opportunity to set up a series of planned learning initiatives to prepare for a larger learning event, such as a webinar or an all-day class. This could be a content refresher or new, general content. Either way, learners will have equal understanding prior to participating in the larger learning event. Preparatory microlearning can be used to supplement and augment training initiatives.

Microlearning can work well in this manner because of the limited interruption it creates to a daily workflow. To prepare for a larger training, the materials can be distributed over time in smaller segments, since taking a five- to 15-minute break to engage in learning is not disruptive to accomplishing daily tasks.

Additionally, the level of knowledge and comprehension on the subject matter will vary depending on the learner's characteristics. But the preparatory microlearning can help to bring everyone up to speed. Then, by focusing on the critical objectives or most complex subject matter during the larger learning event, you can maximize the time of the learners in the room.

As part of their preparatory microlearning content, the Bee Naturals staff are given an overview of the mandated reporting. This will allow the workshop to focus on role plays and demonstrations that bring to life difficult circumstances. The overview includes common terms, regulations, and forms—which are essential components to mandated reporting—to reduce the time needed to explain and review them in person (Table 3-6).

Table 3-6. Preparation-Based Microlearning Example

Use Case	Design Considerations	Contextualized Example	Possible Measures
Preparation	Learner	Staff	• Pre-test
	Content	Mandated reporting (introduction prior to in-person workshop)	• Rubric to evaluate demonstrated knowledge during the workshop
	Content Access	Institution's LMS	
	Development	Explainer video animation	

The Cross Section of Use Cases

In our discussions about microlearning we realized that there will be times when it will be hard to decide which use case is most appropriate. Perhaps the topic and goals sync to more than one. How do you make a choice? This cross section of use cases is not something we want any of you to get caught up on—remember the phrase attributed to Picasso: "Learn the rules like a professional so you can break them like an artist."

So, let's look at performance, preparation, and practice. Getting ready for a presentation based on company standards and how to be successful could be seen as preparatory. However, if the information is available on demand and isn't scheduled like preparation, it is functioning more directly as performance-based microlearning. Why not practice? Answer this: Are you practicing your own presentation or are you setting a presentation up? If it's the latter, we would contend that you are preparing or developing, not practicing, a performance. By asking these questions, you can home in on the use case that best fits your situation.

Use these guiding principles to help you think where and how to best use microlearning in your organization. To assist you further, we've created a worksheet that ties together the prompts and use cases (Figure 3-1). This worksheet will help you map out your ideal microlearning situation and begin to determine (or validate) the use case you want to incorporate.

Figure 3-1. Microlearning Use Case Design Worksheet

| The learning materials will be used to [*choose one*] the training initiative. | ☐ Supplement | ☐ Reinforce |
| | ☐ Augment | ☐ Remediate |

Use Case	Design Considerations	Contextualized Example	Possible Measures
Why do you want to use it? What's the purpose?	Learner	Who are you targeting?	What's the desired performance?
	Content	What subject matter do you want to cover?	
	Content Access	Where do you want to include it? When do you want to incorporate it?	
	Development	What modalities (auditory, visual, etc.) do you want to include?	

Short and Sweet

OK, you've considered the microlearning use cases you are most interested in. You've also taken a moment to complete Figure 3-1 to see how the type and the use case pair for opportunity. Now, how would you implement it?

The final chapter in Section 1 provides additional research to help answer this question. Yes—more research—but we promise it's the good kind. Filling out the worksheet in Figure 3-1 is just the beginning. You have yet to figure out how often you want the microlearning to occur. It seems easy enough, but the way you implement your microlearning can have just as much impact on the learner as its use case and design.

Key Takeaways

Based on the information from this chapter, the following actions will guide how you plan to use your microlearning:

- Microlearning can supplement, reinforce, augment, or remediate a larger training initiative.

- There are six defined use cases for microlearning: pensive, performance-based, persuasive, post-instruction, practice-based, and preparatory.
- Microlearning types refer to the end product that was created, such as videos, podcasts, infographics, and (micro-)e-learning courses.
- Training initiatives rely on a training development infrastructure, which—given team capabilities, desired quality of microlearning product, time, and cost—will also influence what microlearning type is determined.
- Mapping out microlearning initiatives makes it easier to conclude which use case is most appropriate, especially if you think it can fit into more than one use case.

4.
How to Put Microlearning Into Action

Chapter Questions

At the end of this chapter, you should be able to answer these questions:
- What research supports how and when to use microlearning?
- What is the difference between spaced practice and spaced retrieval?
- Can microlearning change a person's behavior?
- What's the optimal length for a microlearning lesson?

In chapter 2, we discussed learning design, supporting our claims with applicable learning theories and domain principles. Then in chapter 3, we used our discussions of how we learn (theories), what we learn (domains), and why we learn (classification) from chapter 2 to help us select the appropriate use case for microlearning.

Now it's time to decide how to put microlearning into action. What provides the best effect? This chapter focuses on taking that use case and incorporating it in a manner that maximizes the outcomes. And we'll share research that can help you understand how to do just that!

To be successful, you need to make sure research and evidence is on your side when you embark on a training or learning initiative. Learning professionals understand that the right application of the right techniques at the right time is what makes a learning program work—not the technique itself. Remember that microlearning is not a panacea in terms of learning design. Without this understanding, you risk wasting organizational resources, not to mention your own time and effort. Use the research and results from the studies in this chapter to inform your implementation of microlearning and to make key decisions about when microlearning will be effective—and when it won't.

Microlearning Research

How far back does microlearning go? The term *microlearning* is typically believed to date back to 2002 (Friesens and Hug 2007). However, even before *microlearning* entered the lexicon, many organizations, teachers, and trainers talked and wrote about chunking learning into small pieces, creating small bites of content, or some other terminology to describe the presentation of small amounts of content to learners. Researchers have studied the presentation of small pieces of content for decades, and there is evidence that the concept of microlearning traces back more than 100 years. There is a large body of research to examine as we describe the application and usefulness of microlearning.

This chapter focuses on a select group of empirical studies and documented research that was approached using sound scientific practices. Our goal was to leverage clear, supported evidence to validate the use of microlearning. Narrowing the body of knowledge to articles that take a scientific approach to microlearning meant that there were fewer resources from which we could draw, but it also removed the "noise" or aspirations for microlearning. Our intent was not to review every study on the subject; rather this chapter aims to provide scientific evidence for the use of microlearning as a tool to deliver instruction.

The Forgetting Curve

In the late 1870s, Hermann Ebbinghaus began to study human memory and, shortly thereafter, the concept of forgetting. Using himself as the subject, Ebbinghaus tirelessly and rigorously experimented with his memory. In 1885 he published a book on the subject titled *Über das Gedächtnis*, which was then translated into English and published as *Memory. A Contribution to Experimental Psychology* in 1913. His study and the publication of his findings was a huge contribution to the study of memory and humankind's understanding of how to improve memory.

The lasting feature of his work is the Ebbinghaus forgetting curve (Figure 4-1), which portrays a plot of memory loss over time. Ebbinghaus found that memories decayed over time. However, he found that when he reintroduced content at certain prescribed intervals, he could diminish the forgetting process.

Ebbinghaus' research has been replicated many times. Researchers Radossawljewitsch (1907) and Finkenbinder (1913) conducted studies similar to Ebbinghaus and found similar results in terms of memory and forgetting. Heller and colleagues (1991) conducted a replication study of Ebbinghaus's work in Germany in the early 1990s. In 2015, Jaap M. J. Murre and Joeri Dros (2015), researchers at the University of Amsterdam, discovered similar results by replicating Ebbinghaus's work as closely as possible, thus rendering the curve valid.

Figure 4-1. Ebbinghaus Forgetting Curve

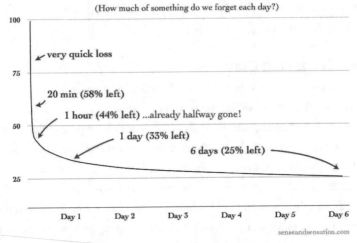

Ebbinghaus' Forgetting Curve

(How much of something do we forget each day?)

very quick loss

20 min (58% left)

1 hour (44% left) ...already halfway gone!

1 day (33% left)

6 days (25% left)

senseandsensation.com

Having stood the test of time (so far), the findings and conclusions of Ebbinghaus clearly indicate that while memory decays over time, that decay can be reduced by reintroducing the items to be learned at specific intervals.

When it comes to using the Ebbinghaus forgetting curve as justification for microlearning, we do have a word of caution: The experiments, even the replicated experiments mentioned here, were all conducted using nonsense syllables as the content to be "learned." Other research has shown that words with specific meanings tend to have more durability than nonsense syllables. So, while the forgetting curve is real, it might not be as applicable to content that has a deeper meaning than nonsense syllables. When the information is more meaningful, the decay or forgetting process should occur more slowly than the Ebbinghaus forgetting curve would indicate. For example, if you needed to learn a series of acronyms at a new job, the forgetting curve would likely not be as steep because those acronyms are related to your job and thus have meaning to you.

It's important to remember that humans do not store information by making a literal copy of that information. Instead, we learn by encoding and storing new information based on how it relates to what we already know. We map new information to current information and link our new information with existing information (Bjork 2012). The introduction of stimuli after an item has been learned will spark memory and aid with retention and recall. In fact, if combined with deeper meaning than nonsense syllables, we can safely assume the forgetting curve will be slowed even more dramatically than Ebbinghaus's work suggests.

In addition to adding meaning, two other types of methodologies can be used to help learners recall information and both can be useful tools as you design microlearning programs. One is called the spacing effect and the other is called the testing effective.

Retrieval: Spaced, Practiced, and Changed Behavior

Much of this chapter is intended to help you determine when and how often to provide learning moments, especially when using microlearning. A little too much information may inundate, demotivate, and even desensitize the learners, and then all your effort would be lost. The research we have pulled together here highlights the best method to use given the use case selected.

As we noted when discussing the forgetting curve, microlearning is great for ensuring our memory is in top condition! So how do we know when to retrieve? Let's look at three different ways we can benefit from retrieval. In the first classification we look at spacing, we then look at opportunities to practice, and, finally, we examine retrieval for impact on behavior.

Spacing

The spacing effect, or spaced retrieval, is an instructional concept that involves providing learners with content spaced over time and has been shown to be an effective tool for aiding retention (Carpenter and De-Losh 2005). It helps to combat learner fatigue, as well as the potential to mix up the preceding and succeeding information they are trying to learn, and typically results in more efficient learning and improved retention (Pashler et. al 2007)

A good way to understand the spacing effect is by focusing on its opposite concept, mass practice. Mass practice is when you study a large body of content all at once, like cramming for a test. Remember doing that? You studied the night before and did really well on the test, but two weeks later you can't remember any of it.

Mass practice or cramming presents two major problems. First is that the successive and preceding content interferes with your ability to learn the new content—concepts will become jumbled and words and definitions won't seem to align. Your brain simply cannot completely understand, memorize, or comprehend the current information before you introduce new information into your memory. The second problem with cramming is simply fatigue. We bet you've studied for a test or tried to learn a great deal of information in one sitting (such as a training workshop or a two-hour webinar), only to find your brain actually "hurting" from trying to absorb too much information. We've certainly felt it.

In short, the spacing effect is based on the fact that memory is enhanced on a delayed test when learning events are distributed in time, rather than massed in immediate succession. The effect works because the act of retrieving information is itself a potent learning event. Retrieved information, rather than being left in the same state it was in prior to being recalled, becomes more recallable in the future; furthermore, competing information associated with the same cues can become less recallable. Using our memories alters our memories (Bjork 2012).

Spaced retrieval is most effective when engaging learners with content over an extended time and when reinforcement of the content is important for learning and application. Research has shown that the greater the amount of spacing between retrieval events, the greater the potential benefit to retention (Dobson 2013). Ideally, you would let more than 24 hours pass between the learning events, but shorter times have also been found to be effective. Learners whose practices were spaced showed better retention even eight years later than those who practiced in a more concentrated time period (Clark and Mayer 2011).

An optimal schedule for spacing content would reactivate information at the exact moment before the information was about to be forgotten by the learner. Since this is virtually impossible to know, it's best to set up a schedule to reintroduce the information. There are two types of schedules associated with the spacing effect (Dobson 2013):

- **The uniform approach.** The information is presented on spaced schedules with an equal amount of time set between learning events. Thus, it's a uniformed spacing approach with a set amount of time between each encounter with the content (Vlach, Sandhofer, and Bjork 2014).

- **An expanding schedule.** The amount of time between learning events gets larger with every presentation of the content (Landauer and Bjork 1978; Vlach, Sandhofer, and Bjork 2014). The spacing interval becomes increasingly longer over the course of the learning period.

Unfortunately, the research does not provide a definitive answer as to the best spacing approach. Some studies indicate uniform is better; others advocate expanded. However, there is a growing body of evidence suggesting that expanding schedules might be superior for individuals or materials that are subject to rapid forgetting (Vlach, Sandhofer, and Bjork 2014). For example, University of Nevada researcher Frank Dempster (1987) found that students retained a higher number of vocabulary definitions when a term and definition were repeated approximately every five minutes, compared with consecutively repeating the same term and definition. There also appears to be a benefit to using spacing within the confines of a single instructional setting.

Recall

Spacing tells *how* learners interact with content; retrieval practice is a type of spacing activity. Because there are different use cases, retrieval practice may not always be part of the mix. However, if we are attempting to practice, reinforce, or remediate, we are inevitably going to need to recall something.

It turns out that retrieving information from memory can be a powerful memory modifier. In other words, recalling information (or testing yourself) modifies the memory trace in a way that increases its accessibility in the future—in other words, it makes it stronger. Quizzing or testing yourself improves learning more than some other forms of encoding, such as restudying (Dobson 2013; Roediger and Karpicke 2006). Thus, while few individuals like them, tests are actually a good way to learn and can play a key role in microlearning.

According to Henry L. Roediger III and Jeffrey D. Karpicke (2006), researchers at Washington University in St. Louis, we can trace the use of testing to aid recall back to at least the 16th century. In a paper titled "The Power of Testing Memory: Basic Research and Implications for Educational Practice," they cite the following from Sir Francis Bacon, the English philosopher and statesman who served as both Attorney General and as Lord Chancellor of England:

> If you read a piece of text through twenty times, you will not learn it by heart so easily as if you read it ten times while attempting to recite from time to time and consulting the text when your memory fails. (F. Bacon 1620/2000, 143; cited in Roediger and Karpicke 2006)

Moving up a few centuries and taking a more scientific approach, Arthur I. Gates (1917) conducted memory experiments at the Psychological Laboratory of the University of California in spring 1916. When studying children from a public school in Oakland, California, and adults who participated at the Psychological Laboratory of Columbia University (Roediger and Karpicke 2006), Gates found that retention was greatly enhanced by testing. His and similar studies have since been replicated, reporting similar results for a variety of learning materials and ages across diverse experimental designs.

Behavior

The spacing effect not only improves recall, it has also been shown to influence a person's behavior. We saw this play out in our example of diabetic patients receiving daily text messages.

In another example, a study titled "Impact on Clinical Behavior of Face-to-Face Continuing Medical Education Blended with Online Spaced Education" found that online spaced education following a live continuing medical education (CME) course significantly increased the impact of the face-to-face course on self-reported global clinical behaviors (Shaw et. al 2011). The randomized controlled trial provided post-instruction microlearning that consisted of quizzing the learner on four clinical topics. Questions were asked every eight and 16 days, based on correct and incorrect responses (spaced retrieval), but the control group wasn't asked any questions until week 18. Both groups were then given a behavior change survey at week 18; those who received the spaced education (microlearning) reported significantly greater change in their global clinical behaviors as a result of the program.

These two examples indicate that the act of spacing information over time and reminding leaners of suggested behaviors and content can have a positive impact on a person's behavior. Thus, when properly employed in a training session, spaced behavioral messages can be used to guide and shape a person's behavior.

This all helps to provide perspective on whether the topic (or topics) you have in mind are well suited for microlearning. Right now, you are probably refining the idea of your microlearning project further by thinking about how you will implement it. But it's probably making you think about the design as well. The biggest question people always have is how long the microlearning should be. Well, there is research to support that as well.

Microlearning Duration

In the definition of microlearning we presented in chapter 1, we purposely avoided assigning a duration because we did not want to artificially constrain the concept of microlearning to a length of time. However, "How long is the right length of time for microlearning?" continues to be a perpetual question we hear.

It should be noted that there is a great deal we don't know about optimal length, such as the relationship between content complexity and length and the relationship between relevancy and the amount of time a person is willing to spend to learn meaningful content. However, there are some research studies that provide insight into the optimal time period for microlearning.

Ralph Burns (1985) conducted research related to the attention span of chemistry students by examining the effect of certain instructional factors and how they related to study recall. He looked at presentation style and order in which ideas were presented to see how they would affect the student's recall of materials.

Here is what he found related to time:

- The learning from the instruction was the greatest during the presentation's first five minutes, with students being able to report about 35 percent of all ideas presented.
- The impact of the presented material declined, but remained relatively constant, for the next two five-minute portions (that is, the next 15 minutes of the presentation).
- The learning impact dropped to the lowest level during the 15- to 20-minute interval.

The findings by Burns and a similar 2013 Harvard study are relatively consistent with other studies related to duration and retention.

Philip Guo, an assistant professor of computer science at the University of Rochester, also found similar results when researching human-computer interactions and online education. He analyzed 6.9 million video-watching sessions in four edX courses, and reported results related to video usage. He found that the optimal length was six minutes or shorter. He also reported that engagement times decreased as the videos become longer. For example, in videos longer than 12 minutes he found students only spent about three minutes watching the video, which means that they viewed less than a quarter of the content (Guo, Kim, and Rubin 2014).

However, Guo also found that when students were earning a certificate, they tended to engage with the videos for a longer period of time than students who were not seeking a certificate. He attributes that to motivation, because those students felt a greater need to watch the videos to eventually earn the certificate.

These recommendations from Guo's research and the findings of others point rather clearly to a five- to six-minute segment, at least for video, of a microlearning lesson. This five-minute mark seems to be gaining consensus within the research community, supported by careful analysis and study. Mind you, this study and others like it were focused on video, and we are not suggesting that their results are representative of all microlearning types. More research is needed to see if there is an optimal overall time length for microlearning in general; we suspect the answer will be "it depends."

Short and Sweet

Much can be gleaned by reviewing research related to the qualities of microlearning. Yes, there is still much to be learned, but you can begin implementing some of these evidence-based results into your own microlearning design and be reasonably assured you are helping the learner. The tips and concepts in this chapter will prevent you from guessing and allow you to present a solid case for why you chose to implement certain elements in your microlearning approach.

This chapter brings section 1 on the foundations of microlearning to a close. By internalizing definitions, theories, domains, use cases, and research, you put yourself and your organization on solid footing when you embark on planning and developing microlearning, the subject of section 2. This will help keep you from being swept up in the microlearning craze and bring a grounded instructional design mindset to preparing how your learners will interact with the content you provide.

Key Takeaways

Based on the findings from the various studies on the elements of microlearning, the following conclusions can be drawn:

- Mass practice or cramming is not effective because the learner can become fatigued.
- Spaced retrieval has been shown to be an effective tool for aiding retention and engaging learners over an extended time.
- Space retrieval is effective when reinforcement of the content is important for learning and application.
- The ideal time between the learning events is greater than 24 hours, but shorter times have also been found to be effective.
- Testing greatly improves retention of material.
- Five minutes appears to be a reasonable length of time for microlearning content.

SECTION 2
PLANNING &
DEVELOPMENT

5.

Creating a Microlearning Strategy

Chapter Questions

At the end of this chapter, you should be able to answer these questions:

- How do I know how and where to incorporate microlearning?
- How can I effectively break down outcomes based on desired behavior and intended use?
- Why is motivation so critical to a microlearning strategy?
- How do delivery methods alter the ability to motivate and elicit the expected performance?

We wouldn't be good ambassadors of making microlearning mighty without giving you a path in the right direction. As you begin to take your vision from macro to micro, it's time to put a plan in place—a microlearning strategy, if you will. Whether you are creating an individual microlearning product or a series of microlearning solutions, you will want to follow a well-designed plan. A plan that matches the intended learning outcome and fits into a larger curriculum while keeping the learner motivated to . . . well . . . learn and, ultimately, change behavior!

ASCE's Strategy for Implementing Microlearning

First, let's start with an example of an organization that's implemented a microlearning strategy. From this example we can divine the strategic microlearning elements they used to help ensure success.

The American Society of Civil Engineers (ASCE) has been the preeminent organization for the civil engineering profession for more than 100 years. The organization, founded in 1852, represents more than 150,000 members in 177 countries and is the nation's oldest engineering society. But like all organizations, ASCE's leadership knew that to remain at the forefront of a profession that plans, designs, constructs, and operates society's economic and social engine, they'd need to rethink how they presented new and existing information to their members.

The challenge was to develop a learning strategy to support ASCE's worldwide members with critical information and learning opportunities related to the global civil engineering standards. These regulations are updated approximately every seven years, and the time to distribute the revisions was fast approaching. The organization conducted a careful needs analysis and determined that the overall deployment strategy would include a new curriculum in a hybrid learning format consisting of live webinar-based instruction, self-paced web content, discussion threads lead by industry experts, and microlearning modules.

The microlearning format was used to help bring together topical content from various subject matter experts within the civil engineering field. These leading experts could provide insights and experiences beyond merely reading the updated standards, and they brought a human element to the content. Because the SMEs' time was highly constrained, the strategy was to equip them with cameras so they could build narrated lessons focused on key points of the content. This approach was chosen because the SMEs were well respected within the field and became a key motivator for learners to participate in the program. The narration from the SMEs was a big hit and brought an air of authenticity to the microlearning lessons.

ASCE determined that the most effective strategy would be a combination of mini-lectures by SMEs, quizzes to help learners recall content, and interactions such as drag-and-drop exercises. These methods helped engage and motivate the learners as they studied and reviewed the content. Due to the need to cover a wide geographical area, the microlearning program was designed for an independent study approach, with each element aligned to the engineering code and delivered over 12 weeks.

Figure 5-1. ASCE's Hybrid Microlearning Curriculum

ASCE AMERICAN SOCIETY OF CIVIL ENGINEERS   Welcome, demo tester | Exit

Earthquake Engineering for Structures

Justin Marshall, PhD, P.E., M.ASCE

⏱ 12:00   0%

This course will discuss why seismic design is important as well as define the underlying principles of seismic hazards analysis, structural dynamics, and inelastic behavior, and examine how seismic design and underlying earthquake principles are integrated into building code requirements.

Live Webinar Dates:
Tuesday, January 30, 2018 @ 3pm, EST
Tuesday, March 13, 2018 @ 3pm, EST

START COURSE ➡

▶ 0:38 / 1:24   🔊

⌄ Week 1: Introduction to Earthquake Engineering for Structures 01:21

This week will cover the motivating factors for performing earthquake design, basic earthquake principles and how these principles are incorporated into the building code. CONTINUE ➡

IN THIS TOPIC: ⊛ EXPERT VIDEO   ∨ KNOWLEDGE CHECK   ↻ REFLECTION

❯ Week 2: Lessons Learned from Previous Earthquakes 01:36

❯ Week 3: Ground Motions and Their Effects 01:43

The microlearning program was well received by ASCE's learners. The just-in-time learning occurred at a pace that worked for busy professionals within the civil engineering field. They could access it when and where they needed. Additionally, the microlearning modules sparked the learners to interact with experts in course discussion threads. Practitioners were so excited about the format and ability to learn from experts that the course was pre-sold and sold out prior to the initial offering. Demand continues to be high to this day.

Your Microlearning Strategy

To begin our discussion of implementing a microlearning strategy, let's start with the underlying assumption that you have or can perform an appropriate training needs analysis and have confirmed opportunities to intertwine microlearning into a larger curriculum, as was done by ASCE. This strategy would most likely include:

- developing an overall goal for the training or learning initiative
- identifying the specific performance indicators for microlearning
- building the use case for microlearning
- creating a profile of the learners.

If you know the delivery platform and format, you will also need to determine the method. If you intend for the initiative to use a new delivery platform (such as an LMS or intranet) or format (such as e-learning courses, video, infographics, or podcasts), deliberating over additional considerations will help you determine the best method.

Your microlearning strategy comprises these three core concepts:

1. mapping outcomes
2. motivating the learner to achieve
3. delivering through an appropriate modality.

The three work together to reciprocally influence the microlearning strategy you design. Consider what happens when you prioritize one over another: A common pitfall is selecting a delivery method (#3) that does not fit into the employee's daily workflow. This makes the learner less inclined to engage with the microlearning product (#2). As a result, your initiative will not meet the mapped outcomes at the level of performance desired (#1). So while they may be motivated and have every intention of engaging with the microlearning product, they may have trouble finding the time because it's outside the normal workflow. Likewise, if the content is highly motivating (#2) and in the workflow (#1) but isn't mapped to needed outcomes (#3), it becomes a waste of time for the individual and the organization. We've seen examples where content delivered via a game is highly motivational, but the content was not relevant to the employee's position and the learning opportunity was wasted. However, everyone continued taking the course because management believed "everyone" should "learn" the content in case it was needed in the future.

Simply put, don't associate the notion of "micro" with "easy" or "rapid." As you can tell from just reading this introduction, the intrinsic reciprocity of each is critical to laying out the best road map to kick off your microlearning endeavors.

You may view mapping outcomes as a perfunctory task, but with microlearning, it needs additional attention. This is because the strategy relies less on mastery of stated learning objectives, and more on mastery of performance. Traditional courses have modules and lessons and even topics that can be or are supported by learning objectives. However, by nature, they allow for broadness of course outcomes and content.

Microlearning is stripped down: One outcome. One to three objectives. This means conciseness. Content must be efficient in its message. Creativity in getting that message across comes with selecting an appropriate vehicle or delivery method that maximizes the learner's motivation.

Now, if your organization already has a microlearning strategy and a series of processes and templates, it is well equipped to move more swiftly in producing additional microlearning products. However, for those that are not versed in incorporating new learning approaches, this chapter provides that foundation.

Making a Microlearning Map

When considering the development of a microlearning strategy, you want to determine where microlearning fits into the overall curriculum. Whether academic or work-related, the curriculum has similar characteristics, which include:

- a learning goal or intent
- a concentrated subject matter area
- a path through the content that builds knowledge or skill acquisition in a logical order
- a learner profile that embodies various characteristics of the targeted group for instruction
- selected instructional strategies and activities, given a chosen theoretical framework, because multiple theoretical approaches can be incorporated (see chapter 3)
- an identified environment and materials

- methods for evaluation
- revision upon analysis of presented data from the evaluation.

Comprehending your curriculum allows you to see the potential use cases for microlearning.

We are not going to cover creating organizational learning strategies, overall curriculums, or rolling out large-scale learning programs, because they are beyond the scope of this book on microlearning. However, there are many books written on those topics, which you can use to help guide you.

We do believe it's important to state that microlearning should not be an afterthought, even if you are using it to supplement existing training or as a resource. You need to know how it fits into the larger learning picture in your organization. Whether formal or informal, microlearning can only be effective if it is part of a larger curriculum. Once you've determined where microlearning fits, the next step is to identify and develop microlearning maps.

As we have encouraged in previous chapters, you should focus on the desired behavior or performance outcome, as opposed to the learning objectives you need to meet. By creating a strategy that dials in on the change you want to elicit, you ensure that the objectives will be met when the learner demonstrates the desired outcome.

To keep the emphasis on the outcome and work toward planning the microlearning initiative, we recommend creating a microlearning map, which is a three-column chart that aligns the outcome, the objectives, and assessment. Table 5-1 shows an example of a microlearning map that might be used in a civil engineering microlearning.

Table 5-1. Microlearning Map for a Bridge Inspection Course

Department: Testing and Control		Job Position: Civil Engineer I	
KPI Group: 1.0 Quality Assurance		Indicator: 1.1 Accuracy and Speed	
Task	**Performance Criteria**		**Objective (no more than 3)**
Inspect a bridge to ensure it meets three critical seismic design criteria.	Given an image of a bridge on the computer screen, the learner will be required to pass or fail the seismic design elements of the bridge with 100% accuracy in 7 minutes.		• Recall the three evaluative criteria. • Recognize if a bridge element should be accepted or rejected.
Intended Use: Reinforcement			

Notice that the map includes the specific curriculum and the targeted KPI (key performance indicator). The first column is the task to be performed: Inspect a bridge to ensure it meets three critical seismic design criteria. Defining the task clearly ensures that the microlearning can be created specifically to address it. The second column specifies the desired outcome from the learner experience, which is the expected performance given the stated KPI group and specific indicator. The goal is that the performance criteria translates to on-the-job performance so that bridges are inspected appropriately. The last column lists the objectives that will be addressed in the microlearning. With these three elements, a specific, focused microlearning program can be created.

Although it may seem backward from typical instructional design approaches for curricular and objective-based mapping, this process is logical given the dialed-in nature of microlearning and our focus on performance. The three-column chart format provides an excellent tool for targeting a behavior and the key content that aligns to achieving it.

Now that we know what we want to see as a success, how do we present the information to the target audience? Given that microlearning has a brief moment to make a large impact, it needs to heavily consider what drives the learner to perform well.

Motivation of the Learner

As an instructional designer, you have a very short amount of time to gain a learner's attention, unleash some amazing content, and help the learner move from learning to doing what they had set out to do. It could be gaining a better understanding of how to speak persuasively to clients, the safety regulations of the workspace, or writing an analytical report. Unless you account for the motivation of the learner, you might end up squandering that the limited amount of time you have to influence them.

In the case of ASCE, one of the motivators was a chance to hear what a recognized industry expert had to say about a subject. In some cases that can be highly motivating. But remember, motivation can mean different things to different people. What should you focus on? As Julie Dirksen (2016) writes in her book *Design for How People Learn,* "There are two kinds of motivation that learning designers need to consider: motivation to learn and motivation to do."

Microlearning ups the ante on motivation. As a result, this section will focus on the motivation to *do,* because microlearning is fantastic for performance improvement (as you know from our umpteenth statement) and that puts us squarely in the affective learning domain. Sure, there are cognitive and psychomotor aspects to learning, but both have a behavioral element based on the motivations of the learner. For example, think about a learner who thinks a safety class is a waste of time, but needs to take it as part of their organization's annual safety requirements. In contrast, another learner needs to take a class to become certified, and thus wants to take that class so they can get promoted. Now, we can think about motivation as a *want* versus a *need:*

- What is the motive of the learner (want)?
- Is the learner's motive influenced by an external demand (need)?

Take, for example, an industry certification exam. The learner is in control of what they want, but they have to want it bad enough. However, even if they want something badly (are highly motivated), a learner can still fail if they:

- didn't believe they could change (self-efficacy)
- were overwhelmed by how much change was involved (expectation setting)
- hadn't reinforced the change with practice or application (self-control).

This seems like a lot to accomplish in any learning format, but even more challenging in a microlearning format. However, it can be done.

Let's look at a real-life example. For the last two years Robyn has been using an app called Elevate, which provides microlearning games as a way to sharpen fundamental skills like math, listening, and reading. The app helps her succeed by influencing her self-efficacy, expectation settings, and self-control:

- **Builds her confidence (self-efficacy).** She sees this through scoring on each game, her accumulated score, level of play (novice, expert, and so on), and even her percentile rank among other users in the same age group. Not only this, but she loves using these skills in a contextualized setting. She feels proud of herself.
- **Increases difficulty over time and provides control over how she engages (expectation setting).** The worked examples allow

her to gain confidence over time and reduce the sense of being overwhelmed. The app is designed to challenge her, but when she is not demonstrating a consistent success rate on a game, the app brings the game's difficulty back down. This way, she can get back to a place where she can "get it" and still feel challenged, not frustrated and overwhelmed. It even has in-game remediation.

• **Offers variation on the same topic and practice (self-control).** With respect to variety, each subject area has alternative games and skills. For example, the math portion has eight different games to allow her to flex her math muscles in a variety of ways. To keep her skills sharp, she practices and reviews study tips, in addition to the daily training session. Plus, when she uses a practice or a tutorial, the app will ask if she wants to set up a reminder in X number of days. For example, she set the app to remind her to practice the eye exercise that strengthens her eye muscles for scanning every three days.

This brain game app does a great job representing the three overarching design principles to encourage a positive behavioral change. These strategies all support the motive of the learner. However, this does not mean that all three must be present. Not everything we learn is overwhelming or beyond our expectations, so we might just focus on helping the learner be more confident in performing their job tasks.

So how do you plan for motivation? One way is to specifically call out how you will motivate the learner. You can use our three column microlearning map as a base, and then modify it to map additional elements. Table 5-2 includes a column for motivation.

Table 5-2. Microlearning Map With Motivational Element

Department: Testing and Control		Job Position: Civil Engineer I	
KPI Group: 1.0 Quality Assurance		Indicator: 1.1 Accuracy and Speed	
Task	Performance Criteria	Objective (no more than 3)	Motivational Element
Inspect a bridge to ensure it meets three critical seismic design criteria.	Given an image of a bridge on the computer screen, the learner will be required to pass or fail the seismic design elements of the bridge with 100% accuracy in 7 minutes.	• Recall the three evaluative criteria. • Recognize if a bridge element should be accepted or rejected.	Make the application of the three criteria into a timed game with seven elements the learner needs to find.
Intended Use: Reinforcement			

Now you are ready to take on the last leg of our strategy: the methods of learning. This is where the interplay of each strategic component can become challenging, based on the approaches taken in delivering the microlearning.

Methods of Learning

As the learner is always the center of any educational product, you want to keep a primary focus on the essential concepts of how to design for their motives. Your design, method, and delivery approach will work together to ensure a sound design aimed at your audience.

For example, Robyn's brain game app is definitely focused on motivating and challenging the user. Part of the reason it works is because the approach is informal. Another part is because it's a game. And still another part is because Robyn has the app on her phone and can conveniently look at it whenever she is early to a meeting or waiting in line at the grocery store.

There are literally dozens of methods for delivering instruction, including gamification (Karl's favorite), short sims, and infographics (we'll talk about them in depth in chapter 7). It's also important to note that often the motivational aspect (such as a game) overlaps with the method, which can also be a game, like in Robyn's brain game app.

But regardless of specific method, it's about understanding the characteristics of each method and evaluating how they will assist or limit opportunities to motivate the learner. A particularly broad way of looking at microlearning methods is to consider formal versus informal, or push versus pull delivery.

Formal vs. Informal Learning

We'll cut to the chase here and discuss the key attributes of the two approaches, formal and informal, through a comparison chart (Table 5-3). These characteristics will help you:

- Define the environment if you are uncertain of what kind it is.
- Determine if there are limitations to the approach, given what you want the learner to accomplish.
- Consider the possibilities and opportunities within the learning method that will strengthen the motivation of the learner.

These two environments embrace the idea of push versus pull. Formal learning approaches most commonly push content to the learners. A pull environment, on the other hand, is one that the learners develop for themselves by locating materials and resources. Depending on how the formal learning environment was set up, the learners may also be able to pull formally created content when they need it.

Table 5-3. Comparing Formal Versus Informal

Formal Learning	Informal Learning
Goals are set by someone else.	Goals are individually based and individually guided.
Learning is available only during fixed times. The learning content is pushed to the learner.	Learning is available 24/7. The learner accesses or pulls the content when they want it. They seek information or content in manners that work for their way of learning.
The content is structured for the learner by someone else.	The learner creates a structure and works toward gathering information to fit that structure.
Content is developed and distributed by someone else or delivered by a professional as opposed to a peer.	Content and information are gathered from peers. The learner and their peers share their know-how among themselves.
The content is consistent in message and validated for accuracy.	The content and information are unpredictable. The accuracy, level of credibility, and relevance of the content are not controlled.
Learner must determine how to best learn the material as opposed to selecting the learning methods they know will work best for them.	Learner adapts to the content by creating their own learning environment.
Learning is typically scheduled, or time needs to be set aside to engage with the content. This can take away from other work.	Learning is usually organic, occurring when time is available or at time of need. Learning can happen every day if the learner chooses.
Costlier to develop.	Usually inexpensive.

For example, a company put on an in-person training session (push/formal) on effective management skills, which Mary attended. The company also posted the materials from the face-to-face class on its training SharePoint site. Mary can now access that content when she wants (pull/informal). Likewise, she can ask her co-worker for advice as she strengthens her management skills (pull/informal), and she can sign up to get weekly tips on being an effective manager (push/formal) from human resources.

If you are versed in the push/pull perspective of learning, you will recognize some common characteristics. For example, push is denoted as a top-down approach and pull as bottom-up. Also, push is more instructor-centered, while pull is more learner-centered. However, in the informal learning example with Mary, we note a bottom-up approach because she selected to receive the formal learning. Additionally, the weekly tips from HR were not instructor-centered; instead, the content was designed to help managers hone their managerial skills, but it was an option, not a requirement.

This is not to say that the definitions and associated attributes for push and pull learning are inaccurate. In the situation with Mary, she exemplifies the key points mentioned at the beginning of this section:

- **Defining the environment.** Mary has chosen an informal environment, but the learning setting is at work, through and with peers, and with learning assets provided by human resources.
- **Determining if there are limitations to the approach given what you want the learner to accomplish.** Human resources may have determined that learning management skills all at once in a formal setting may not elicit the anticipated outcome of having more effective managers.
- **Considering the possibilities and opportunities within the learning method that will strengthen the motivation of the learner.** Following through from the last point, human resources saw an opportunity to introduce new concepts to managers in a relatively informal way, while still controlling the message and content. In addition, sending a tip a week can be motivational to the learner from a self-efficacy and self-control perspective.

Once you understand the push versus pull delivery options, you can start to look at the specific methods and make intelligent decisions about the right instructional design approach for microlearning. Table 5-4 shows an additional column on the map that indicates the desired method for the microlearning delivery (specific methods will be covered in chapter 7).

Table 5-4. Microlearning Map With Learning Method

Department: Testing and Control		Job Position: Civil Engineer I		
KPI Group: 1.0 Quality Assurance		Indicator: 1.1 Accuracy and Speed		
Task	Performance Criteria	Objective (no more than 3)	Motivational Element	Method
Inspect a bridge to ensure it meets three critical seismic design criteria.	Given an image of a bridge on the computer screen, the learner will be required to pass or fail the seismic design elements of the bridge with 100% accuracy in 7 minutes.	• Recall the 3 evaluative criteria. • Recognize if a bridge element should be accepted or rejected.	Make the application of the 3 criteria into a timed game with 7 elements the learner needs to find.	• Informal • Game
Intended Use: Reinforcement				

Short and Sweet

Following the process of creating a microlearning map, adding a column for motivation, and determining the right method provides a solid start for creating your microlearning strategy. We've seen microlearning maps that are highly detailed and maps that are relatively simple. The key is to create your map at a level that helps your organization focus on meeting the goals of the instruction. This planning seems like a lot of work upfront, but that work pays off with a smooth implementation. This is especially critical if it's a multiple year curriculum. So, take the time to plan your strategy and the other pieces will fall into place.

Once you have the strategy ready, the next step is to think about the implementation.

Key Takeaways

Based on the information from this chapter, the following actions will guide your microlearning strategy:

- For microlearning to be an effective element within an organization, it often takes more planning than traditional instruction, not less.
- Your microlearning strategy comprises three components:
  - mapping the performance to the task and determining the use case for the identified learning
  - recognizing that motivational strategies are critical given the short duration of "seat time" of microlearning
  - selecting the method or methods of delivery for your microlearning products.
- When examining the formality of the microlearning, define the environment in which the learning will take place.
- Determine if there are limitations to the microlearning approach given what you want the learner to accomplish.

6.
Planning and Implementing Microlearning

Chapter Questions

At the end of this chapter, you should be able to answer:

- What project factors influence the planning and implementation of microlearning?
- Why is an implementation plan for microlearning critical for success?
- What are the stages of production that comprise a microlearning development process?
- How do risk and change management influence project planning?
- What variables should be considered when calculating development time for creating microlearning?

As seasoned practitioners, we know all too well the calamities that befall poorly planned training initiatives. We also know that not all learning and development professionals come to their job roles the same way. That's why the topic of planning and implementing microlearning initiatives is so vital. On one extreme, we have people with a blank slate who have never tried microlearning, although they may have had other experiences in managing, planning, or participating in a training project. On the other, are the folks who gave microlearning a shot but felt burned by the effort.

Somewhere in the middle resides the sweet spot all managers of learning initiatives strive for—low risk, few changes in project expectations, a committed team, and a well-estimated timeline. Oh, and a stable budget with a little padding. But until you can consistently get this unicorn and rainbows mix, you should take what you know and reflect on it with the considerations we raise in this chapter.

Although it should go without saying, we want to be clear that our perspective is based on:
- industry best practices
- our own years in the field and in performing research
- what we believe are unique aspects of microlearning that influence the planning and implementation of it.

Failco's Unsuccessful Microlearning Implementation

We can learn a great deal from failure. So let's look at a company that had a "not so successful" microlearning implementation. Names, locations, and other details have been changed, but the underlying reasons for failure and miscues by management are all too real.

This company (called Failco—an attempt at a cute name) is a manufacturing organization located somewhere in northwest United States. The company had been manufacturing furniture for decades and had a solid product. Unfortunately, sales were down and many in the company attributed the lack of sales to the new sales force who had not "grown up with the products." Therefore, they needed more training.

In a desperate search for ideas, the assistant vice president of sales at Failco attended a short webinar on the virtues of microlearning. Upon hearing of some impressive sales increase percentages during the webinar, he decided immediately that microlearning was the solution to the sales department's problem. His first step was to order the training department to "chop up" existing e-learning sales modules into smaller pieces, which were called "bite-sized learning."

The problem was that the courses couldn't just be "chopped up." The one-person training department needed to apply some instructional design practices to the pieces or they wouldn't make a great deal of sense. In addition, since the project was undertaken with such desperation and no planning, no one really knew what the budget was. So, with management's full attention on microlearning, the one-person training department saw this sudden interest and the growing demand for instructional designers as a chance to hire more employees. Within a month, three new employees were added to the training department.

The head of quality heard about the microlearning initiative and decided to purchase an off-the-shelf microlearning library of Lean Six Sigma courses. She had always wanted to implement Lean Six Sigma but could never get buy in. However, she hoped that having the modules would help improve the organization and, perhaps, get momentum moving in her direction. Unfortunately, she hadn't asked the IT department to vet the microlearning courses, which, it turned out, were optimized for mobile devices and not desktop stations. In fact, the presentation on a desktop looked rather anemic. The problem was that the people working on the floor did not have company mobile devices and were highly reluctant to download the software on their private phones. So they had to take a few minutes before or after their shifts to go to a desktop and take the Lean Six Sigma training. As you can imagine, morale was horrible because the training looked bad and the organization wasn't even undertaking a Lean Six Sigma initiative. It seemed to most of the employees to be a colossal waste of time.

In the meantime, the AVP of sales didn't bother to conduct a pilot program before he rolled out the sales-related microlearning to all 56 sales professionals. Once again there were technology issues—the program ran well on the iOS phones, but didn't run well at all on the Android phones. The company had allowed sales reps to purchase whatever phone they wanted, and it was an almost even split. Half the sales force had no access to the microlearning.

Four months later the AVP of sales was fired along with the entire training staff because of their "out-of-control budgets," "lack of results," and poor estimates of how long the project would take. It was an unmitigated disaster.

Factors Influencing Planning and Implementation

The Failco microlearning disaster was a direct result of poor planning, no recognition of the many factors that influence the success of microlearning, and an out-of-control spending spree. Unfortunately, these types of microlearning implementation failures are more common than they should be.

One thing that leads to disaster is not accounting for the many variables that need to be considered when implementing microlearning, such as the organization's work environment, culture, technology infrastructure, and experience launching learning programs. Yes, Failco saw the potential of microlearning, but the training department should have raised a red flag when it realized that it was simply being used as a way to quickly enhance training and increase sales. There was a complete lack of planning or coordination within the organization.

Now you might not be in the same situation as Failco, and we recognize that our readers are coming from different starting points. You could be updating an existing training program or launching a new product or teaching college seniors about game design. Not all situations are the same, but the basic process is and following it will help you avoid many mistakes.

For example, a new initiative would require a longer runway for implementation. Not only because there will be unforeseen circumstances, but other factors, like resistance to change by stakeholders, will add risk. This in turn would create a need to plan additional activities in preparation for implementation, such as a marketing campaign or informational sessions to answer questions.

Meanwhile, in a company where microlearning has been part of the corporate culture for many years, implementing a new "flavor" of microlearning, such as a gamified approach or adding videos, won't be as big a shock to the organization.

Of course, different microlearning types, modalities, and use cases will also factor into your implementation process. We've outlined a process here that will likely require some modifications, but the basic framework is solid and can be used in virtually any type of microlearning implementation. Your job is to take the information from the other chapters in this book, combine it with the framework presented here, and make an effective plan.

But to paraphrase an old military saying, "No plan survives contact with the reality of implementing microlearning."

Getting Started With Planning and Implementation

With that thought in mind, where should you start? Great question. We will approach planning and implementation based on a training development process that looks at the three stages of production: pre-production, production, and post-production.

Before moving forward, we need to define what we mean by the *training development process*. To us, it encompasses the activities and respective methods used to create a learning product. This process includes the initial planning to the kick-off meeting to the implementation or launch of the product for use by the learning audience, all the way through executing the evaluation plan.

Pre-Production

Pre-production is considered the planning phase for developing and implementing the learning product, which, in this case, is microlearning. Activities to undertake at this stage should include, but are not limited to:

- defining the project scope with the client (who can be internal or external to your organization); for example, expectations, budget, timeline, resources, and assumed risks
- analyzing the learners, the learning environment, technical specifications, tasks, and instructional goals
- assessing any previously developed learning materials
- gathering content and other subject matter–based materials
- defining a creative direction
- determining resources (such as equipment and talent) and methods of acquisition.

Use your best judgement to decide which activities are of the most value and resonate within your organization. However, don't spend so much time in pre-production that you never reach production—be intelligent about how deep and how much analyzing, planning, and defining you need to perform. You need to do some, but you don't need to write a tome either.

Production

Production is the actual creation and development of all the learning assets. During this phase, the main goal is to keep to the agreed timeline, gain approval from the client (internal or external), and mitigate risk. An undercurrent that runs parallel to creating the microlearning product is the implementation tasks.

Implementation activities can even commence in pre-production if necessary. For example, to test a new microlearning product on the organization's intranet, the IT department would want to ensure an appropriate environment is set up and ready for testing. This might mean something simple, like creating a new folder structure, or it could be something more complex, like upgrading the intranet platform, adjusting settings on the server to play back different file types, or ensuring appropriate plug-ins are in place.

Pilot testing may even need to start months before actual training development of the microlearning (production phase). This can happen if you're trying a complex solution, like a mobile app, or coordinating the timing to other types of learning events. For example, we cannot imagine sending out 52 educational email messages as a microlearning initiative without first creating some type of prioritization process to determine when you would distribute them. You certainly would not want to release them all at once! You would also need to work with IT to distribute the messages to the appropriate audiences and to manage the distribution lists. And, depending on the content and your organization, each message may need to be approved by the legal department.

Even aspects that occur post-implementation can require more time than just what you would have during production. For example, part of implementation may be gaining usage data (such as open rates and click through counts) from those 52 emails. If your current email software does not offer these types of analytics, the organization may also need to research, request bids, purchase, test, and pilot an analytics tool.

Post-Production

The post-production phase starts when you have scheduled the microlearning objects (if there is more than one) to deploy. The phase ends with implementation of the entire initiative, which includes, but is not limited to:

- testing or piloting the training
- marketing the new training as necessary (such as for compliance)
- training helpdesk and technical staff (as applicable)
- rolling out the finalized product to the target audience
- evaluating the deployed training.

With respect to evaluation, microlearning creates a lot of buzz around how effective it can be. In chapter 4 we explored research that shared compelling evidence of its ability to influence performance outcomes when designed and deployed in an effective manner. With that in mind, we believe that those interested in investing time in microlearning will evaluate the effectiveness of not only the products, but also the processes used to create the microlearning products. We take a deeper dive into evaluation on both fronts in chapter 8.

Risk and Change Management

Why is it that risk comes first when change is to blame? It's like when you know you have to invite an acquaintance to your party—not because you want to, but because they will inevitably find out about it. That's change. But when that acquaintance decides to bring an uninvited guest? That's risk.

In new initiatives, change is typically the front runner to the issue of risk. Key factors are:

- unforeseen issues—we don't know what we don't know
- budget—we underestimate projected hours for each or all phases
- implementation—we didn't give ourselves enough time to flesh out the infrastructure or technology
- lack of buy-in from project stakeholders.

Granted, risk can happen aside change. For example, your SME just got promoted and is leaving for a month to begin an intense management program. Sure, there will be change, but this is less an anticipated change and more so a common factor for general project risk. Again, organizational culture may factor into whether it is a perceived risk. If the organization's culture is big on employees moving into other roles and promoting from within, this is an acceptable and anticipated change. It would be seen as low risk given that it's commonplace.

The same goes for our previous discussion points on implementation—a well thought out implementation plan provides low risk, but the more change necessary for successful implementation, the higher the risk. Common challenges with microlearning implementation revolve around resources and the ability to sustain the solution—especially if the microlearning initiative is a scheduled event. You will need to plan all microlearning initiatives for distribution based on the flow and timing of the overarching learning initiative (Figure 6-1).

Figure 6-1. The Balance Between Low and High Risk

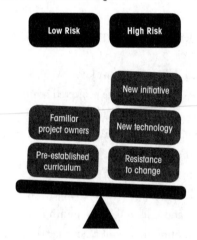

Let's take a look at an onboarding program that has undergone an evaluation to reduce turnover and increase job performance in the first three months. Part of the augmented program leverages microlearning through a combination of scheduled emails, videos, podcasts, and (micro-)e-learning courses. Given the new hire's job role, some of the videos and e-learning modules will be different, whereas the emails and podcasts will be the same for everyone.

As part of planning, you recognize that you will need more involvement from marketing to assist in crafting the emails and podcasts. You will also need more support from IT to help define the user groups and align the content to those user groups to push the correct content at the right time. IT is also concerned about video playback and needs to perform tests for load and bandwidth, because previous training sessions did not include video or podcasts.

Next, you realize you need to adjust and expand your efforts in tracking and monitoring the release of the training program. Additionally, you need to devise a development schedule that maximizes the creation of the new learning components because the internal training department's bandwidth was tapped and a vendor is being contracted. Selecting the contractor will also take time because you'll need to go through the appropriate channels for procurement.

We could keep going, but we hope you get the picture: A little (micro) change can have a big impact on resources.

Sustainment and Maintenance

Even with pre-production, production, and post-production considerations, your microlearning planning process should include other considerations. A particularly important aspect of microlearning to consider is how you plan to maintain the content. Often microlearning is served in small pieces over a long period of time and you need a maintenance plan to avoid repetition and obsolescence of content, and to keep up with changes. At the very least, you should know ahead of time when you are planning to "retire" the microlearning and implement other content.

We would be remiss if we didn't highlight this need to consider the maintenance aspects of your microlearning initiative. Our research and experience with clients show that while implementation is addressed in project planning, it is only to the point of getting the training to its new digital home and making sure the door is unlocked for learners. These plans commonly leave out any instructions for the maintenance or sustainment of a training solution.

Returning to the onboarding program example: It clearly has a maintenance element that is more than just plug-and-play. Company polices may change, company logos may change, the information you want to tell new employees may change. You need to have a plan for how to update the content and maybe even the technology. In fact, while you are planning to maintain and sustain the microlearning modules over time, it also might be a good time to think about how you are going to evaluate your microlearning program. We'll talk more about that in chapter 8, but that doesn't mean you shouldn't start thinking about evaluation early.

At this point, you might be asking if evaluation planning fits under sustainment or maintenance. Or is it implementation? Well, it's kind of all three. If you don't think about evaluation at the implementation stage or determine how you are going to deliver and update the microlearning content, then it might be too late to set up your evaluation process later on. You might not have the right protocols or links set up to collect the data you want to ensure the microlearning efforts are hitting the mark.

Evaluative measures need to be determined early so data input opportunities can be identified. This will inform you of where and when to implement evaluation. However, once implemented the evaluative approach will also need sustained. With the onboarding example, your team will be pushing emails and other microlearning to the learners. As a result, from the training side, data would be pushed to you at identified times as part of evaluative approach. If systems or APIs change, then changes need to be made to the process for pushing data.

Estimating Microlearning Hours

Now, once you've nailed down planning factors such as production, risk, and maintenance, it's time to think about developing the microlearning. The big question then becomes: How long does it take to develop microlearning? How much time do you need to plan for the design and development? The standard and not very satisfying answer is, *it depends.*

This answer is based on research we have published every few years since 2003, focused on how long it takes to develop an hour of training. Our latest update to the research was in 2017. Now, we won't say that estimating development hours for microlearning or any learning is our favorite task, but we have gained a number of insights into what affects the time requirements for development.

To start, you want to consider your level of experience in training development, the use of the ADDIE model (analyze, design, develop, implement, and evaluate), if you've got a contracted resource or an internal department, and whether you're using templates and style guides. If that wasn't enough, you should also look at what influences the developmental hours. Several of those factors also align with risk and change management. Our work has shown that the most critical influences on estimating hours are:

- a clear plan that is understood equally by all project stakeholders
- buy-in from all project stakeholders

- comprehension of the expected outcomes, responsibilities, and tasks by both project stakeholders and supporting staff
- established development processes including standard development and review cycles, templates, and style standards
- consistent and timely communications
- an agreed-upon plan for managing project scope changes and modifications.

These broad areas cover much of what causes problems with a project that's underway; however, we are not claiming that these are the only variables. Use them as guiding principles and evaluate each against the knowns of your organization to factor their weight upon project planning.

If you want to get more precise about estimating the exact amount of time it might take to develop microlearning, you'll need to roll up your sleeves and create an hours estimate. To create an estimate, there are four basic methods: similar projects, formulas, bottom up, and industry standards.

One thing to keep in mind with estimating—it almost always takes longer to develop microlearning than you anticipate. Don't be lulled by the term "micro."

Similar Projects

Think about projects you've already done that are similar to the current microlearning you need to develop. Consider this scenario: Have you ever done microlearning before? *No.* Are you trying to create a video? *Yes.* Have you done video for other learning initiatives? *Yes.* Well then, same rules apply. Just because it's micro doesn't mean that the process will be any different to develop video. Use what you know to help estimate.

A word of caution: Don't fall into the following logic. You know that it takes 100 hours of time to develop one hour of e-learning in your company. The microlearning module is only six minutes, which is a tenth of an hour, so you think you'll only need 10 hours of development time. Not true! The shorter learning time does not necessarily equate to a shorter development time. For example, it takes just as long to set up a shoot to capture one hour of live action video as it does to capture six minutes; the set-up time doesn't change even if the recording time does. Also, it's often more difficult and time consuming to create a short, highly focused learning piece than a rambling one-hour module of a SME's mind dump. In fact, when Karl's grandmother sent him long letters in college, she would apologize by quoting Mark Twain: "I didn't have time to send you a short letter, so I wrote you a long one."

The underlying premise is that *this* project is analogous to *that* project. This type of estimating is used when you don't have a lot of information about the current project or when two projects appear to be similar. Of course, if they appear to be similar but aren't actually, the estimate will not be accurate. This method tends to be better for creating a ballpark estimate rather than an actual estimate.

Formulas

Another estimation technique is approximating the number of hours it might take based on experience and then applying weights for different factors. This is a process similar to the one described by Lou Russell in *Project Management for Trainers* (2015). A weighted factor is used to compensate for things like expertise. Obviously, an expert instructional designer might take a little less time than a novice, so it makes sense that you'd want to factor that into the equation.

The fancy term for this type of estimation is called Parametric modeling (Kapp 2003). The design and development variables are assigned a weight based on a number of factors including:

- expertise—your or your team's familiarity with instructional design and content
- project-related work—the amount of time added to an activity to account for the number of people working on the activity (it always takes more time when you have more people on a project)
- level of interactivity within the microlearning product
- environment—factors that are not direct production hours, like checking email or attending client meetings.

If you are interested in more details on this method of estimating time, we strongly recommend tracking down Russell's book on project management for trainers or Karl's book *Winning E-Learning Proposals*, which contains a chapter on the subject.

Bottom Up

Another type of estimation is a bottom-up estimation, or what is sometimes referred to as a work breakdown structure (WBS). Bottom-up estimating is a process by which the major deliverables are broken down into smaller tasks until each task can be easily assigned a time value. The idea is that if you can break down each microlearning piece into a series of definable tasks and then assign an estimate, you can roll up all the tasks to determine how long it will take for the entire microlearning project. This is perhaps one of the most accurate methods for determining the amount of time to create microlearning, but the process itself is time consuming.

Also, keep in mind that while this method can be effective, it's not perfect. If a task is forgotten or time is not included for communication among team members or someone severely over or underestimates a task, the estimation can be inaccurate.

Industry Standards

Using an industry benchmark can be helpful if you've never developed microlearning before or if you want to gain some understanding of whether your development times are above or below average. For example, if you know that most organizations take 50 hours to develop a 10-minute microlearning lesson, then you can gauge approximately how long that might take you. Unfortunately, since no universal standards have been sanctioned by a governing body, exact standards do not exist.

Phil Mayor, creative director at eLearning Laboratory, suggested it would take around three hours to develop (information gathering, design, authoring, and so on) any learning program under eight minutes. If the microlearning was longer than eight minutes, he said to add an additional hour of development time for each minute. As an example, if the e-learning seat time was nine minutes, you should estimate that it would take you four hours to develop. You would need three hours for initial development of the first eight minutes and an additional hour for the ninth minute (Westin 2017).

This formula accounts for the initial heavy lifting or "set up" of designing and developing instruction regardless of the ultimate instructional length. The setup cost is fairly consistent if you are shooting only two minutes of video, because you still need a camera, scripts, and lighting. All those elements have costs and time requirements that won't change whether a shoot is eight minutes or eight hours—the duration of the instruction is simply the additional time and cost over and above the set up (which is accounted for in the first eight minutes).

Others have suggested that inputting content into a template-driven microlearning tool can take as little as two minutes. That's great for inputting content, but it provides no information about the level of effort to gather the content, design the content, choose the right instructional strategies, and then write or otherwise create the content. As of this writing, there are no hard and fast industry guidelines specifically for microlearning development. So, estimating the exact hours it will take to develop a piece of microlearning is still as much an art as it is a science.

Short and Sweet

Properly implementing microlearning can be thought of as a multistep process involving pre-production, production, and post-production as well as considerations of risk and the long-term maintenance of microlearning content. One big part of the entire process is to determine the number of hours it will take a team to develop the necessary microlearning. There are many factors that influence the length of time; we've listed many in this chapter but there are always others. The important thing to note is that you should choose an estimation method and use that method consistently to develop a real sense of the numbers that work for your organization.

Following the steps in this chapter should help you have a smooth implementation with few surprises. The more you can anticipate factors that might negatively impact progress, the better you are able to mitigate that risk. Even if your estimate is not 100 percent accurate (and it won't be), simply thinking through the factors and understanding the potential risks will better prepare you for the microlearning development process.

Key Takeaways

Based on the information from this chapter, the following actions will guide the planning and implementation of your microlearning initiative:

- A multitude of variables influence the project, and you should consider as many as possible when planning. For example, culture or organization, current work processes, and current technological infrastructure.
- Microlearning can seem like a quick and easy solution to implement, but it is also important to consider that most microlearning projects need more consideration around planning and implementation. Although all training initiatives should consider implementation up front, microlearning projects have a higher risk if implementation is not discussed for pilots and new initiatives.
- One method of breaking down a microlearning project into a workflow is to use a production mindset. Pre-production is used for planning; production is the actual process of creating and developing; and post-production is where implementation and evaluation reside.
- With any new initiative there is inherent risk and change to manage. Implementing and sustaining microlearning can create some of the greatest risks and changes to different departments, especially to workflow and human resources.

- There are too many variables to list when calculating development time, but they can usually be grouped by expertise of the training developer and expertise in the subject matter, number of people on the project, the administrative aspects of projects for purposes of management and moving work forward.
- There are several options for estimating project hours.
- Estimating the exact amount of time it takes to create microlearning is still as much of an art as it is a science.

7.
Designing Microlearning

Chapter Questions

At the end of this chapter, you should be able to answer these questions:

- How does the way I write influence my microlearning product? What writing style should I use?
- How do I write valuable multiple-choice questions to include in my microlearning program?
- What are some best practices for creating video or audio-based microlearning?
- How does the layout and visual design affect my microlearning product?
- How does storyboarding help manage layouts and aesthetics in microlearning?
- What methods can be used to make microlearning engaging?

Classroom instruction comes in many forms—lectures, facilitated discussions, hands-on demonstrations, question and answer sessions, and small group exercises, just to name a few. We tend to lump a great deal of delivery approaches under the umbrella of "classroom" instruction.

The same is true for microlearning. There are many ways of delivering microlearning, from podcasts to infographics.

This chapter discusses design considerations for various microlearning delivery methods that can help create engaging content. We weren't sure what type of microlearning you'd be developing, so we provided tips ranging from video-based lessons to text-based considerations. This chapter is not exhaustive in terms of design guidelines or methods. Instead, it's meant to get you started and to help you think about the creation of microlearning events. Entire books have been written on creating video or podcasts, so don't expect every last detail. Instead, we'll cover just enough to get you started. Where you go from there is up to you.

NBC Universal Matches Microlearning Design With Need

Here is a case study illustrating how NBC Universal (NBCU) leveraged microlearning to help improve speaking skills within the organization. The talent development team at NBCU used a practice-based microlearning app called Presentr to help individuals at the organization improve their presentation skills. Their use of the app was so successful that they have begun deploying it in several areas of the organization. The case highlights how the right design elements helped make the app attractive to the users. The elements of this case study are applicable whether you are developing an app yourself or, like NBCU, you are evaluating apps to meet your needs. The design elements are critical to successful microlearning. You need to identify necessary design elements and seek a solution that contains them. The content in this chapter will help you identify microlearning that has been well designed and also design effective microlearning.

NBCU, owned by Comcast, is one of the most well-known media companies in the world. The company, which has more than 62,000 employees globally, comprises various media properties including NBC, MSNBC, CNBC, Bravo, the Golf Channel, the Weather Channel, Telemundo, and Universal Studios.

The NBCU talent development team provides many leadership development opportunities for its employees. One of those programs focuses on how to be influential, where participants pitch an idea to their peers and ultimately one of their bosses. In earlier sessions of this program, the participants would pitch their peers and receive peer-to-peer feedback. However, this exercise proved challenging because the peer group thought they lacked the objective expertise to provide the appropriate feedback. Without the appropriate feedback, it is hard to improve presentation skills. So the NBCU team decided to find a training solution to the feedback problem.

The program on influence is broken out over several months and participants are spread out around the country. The cohort is only brought together for live training twice. This lack of face-to-face opportunities meant that any solution had to be app-based, self-paced, and conducted in short sessions. And, since the participants would have to fit practice in during their normal workday, microlearning became an important component. Practicing speaking or preparing for a presentation should not be done in long sessions, because the learner can become overwhelmed and more self-critical.

The solution NBCU sought had to hit the right levers to be adequate. They wanted something that was mobile, allowed for short practice sessions, provided feedback, and tracked participant development. The users had to be able to effectively improve their skills and walk away feeling that the five, 10, or 15 minutes they invested provided insights and improved their understanding, confidence, and, most importantly, ability to effectively convey a message. It also needed features and functionality that made it easy to use.

NBCU looked at several off-the-shelf solutions but eventually chose Presentr, a mobile communication skills coach that allows users to learn, practice, and improve their skills in short sessions. In short, the app contained all the design elements they required.

The concept behind Presentr is that it's like having an on-demand coach providing customized support to people learning to present. It has gamification elements such as timers and even some actual games to keep the learners focused. It also uses instructional videos that can be accessed based on any performance weaknesses defined by the app. This allowed participants to engage in microlearning events specifically targeted to their learning needs.

NBCU provided participants with subscriptions to the app at the beginning of the influence development program, and then sent weekly reminders and recommended practice activities.

Within the app, participants were able to practice several skills. They could record themselves speaking and receive a score based on volume, pacing, and frequency of filler words. This provided a baseline of their presentation skills. The next step was practice. The app determined which areas were strong and which required more work, offering games and gauges to help users improve their skills. Users could type in their frequently used filler words or phrases and have the app count how many times they said them in a presentation. The app also provided tips and techniques through video-based microlearning lessons.

The app's easy-to-read dashboard feature allowed the talent development team to monitor app use and engage with the users to remind them to practice. Participants could use the app on their mobile phones and laptops, and they received virtual onboarding for the program.

Throughout the first year Presentr was implemented, six cohorts (approximately 250 users in total) used the app as part of their development program. The general feedback was positive, although adoption was initially mixed across the cohorts. However, with the encouragement of the talent development team, more and more people used the app and were able to drive stronger engagement with the microlearning.

With positive results, NBCU decided to support this approach for future training programs and is also looking at other areas of the business to utilize this technology. Additionally, a leadership team at Telemundo in San Diego has decided to give their team access to microlearning through Presentr.

Following Sound Design Principles

As you can see from this case study, the microlearning app was designed specifically with elements such as gamification and instructional videos to help learners gain the required skills. The app followed sound design principles to make the microlearning effective, which enabled NBCU employees to improve their skills.

While microlearning is a great tool for learning, it can sometimes be difficult to encourage learners to interact with it regardless of format. Fortunately, there are techniques that you can use to make microlearning engaging. Of course, the first method is to have compelling content that the learner needs to know. This can be a great motivator. However, when an organization is teaching compliance or a student is memorizing content for a quiz, the information may not be as compelling as one would hope.

You need to follow sound design principles when creating your microlearning program. You might not be implementing something as interactive as Presentr, but you still need to design with engagement and quality in mind. This chapter provides a high-level view of some of the principles used by Presentr as well as other design guidelines to help you create the most effective microlearning. It tackles writing style, podcasting, graphic layout and aesthetics, video, gamification, short sims, and storyboarding.

Writing Style

We hazard that you have all heard of Keep It Short and Simple (K-I-S-S). Right? No matter what type of microlearning you are developing (job aid, podcast, video), this is a great design principle to keep in mind. Minutes matter but conveying a concise message can prove challenging, especially if you are familiar with the content and subject matter. There are two areas where you can concentrate your energy to keep your writing dialed in: create concise, active scripts and use questions to focus the learner on the content that matters.

Concise Scripting

When you script the content for a microlearning lesson you want to make sure that it's not long-winded or heavy in explanation. Hello K-I-S-S! Keep it short and to the point. Unfortunately, wordiness can become a problem when creating a microlearning script. You want to avoid the desire to impress the learner and just stick with the information that conveys your message. Extra words can clutter sentences and hide meaning, so make a concentrated effort to "trim" words and avoid complexity (Kapp 2003). Table 7-1 shows a few wordy phrases and suggestions to shorten them.

Table 7-1. Examples of Wordy and Concise Phrases

Wordy Phrase	Concise Phrase
Absolutely essential	Essential
Advance notice	Notice
Ahead of schedule	Early
A large number of	Many
At the present time	Now
Many different ways	Many ways
Puzzling in nature	Puzzling

Once you start to trim phrases and focus on the content that exemplifies the core of the message, how can you set up your writing to keep that laser focus? Try the following approach:

- **Set it up.** This is your overview sentence, which provides the broadest statement to your presented content. Think 100 percent.
- **Elaborate.** This is where you drill down to the specific point or points. Think 80 percent.
- **Give an example (as needed).** This is straightforward—it places the second sentence in a context relevant to the learner. Depending on the second sentence, you may need to provide an example.

Your message will look something like this:

Having a technique to rely on to mitigate unexpected conflict is critical to diffusing the situation quickly. *[Set Up]* Create your own approach by using PRISM: Put the meeting on pause, Remove uninvolved peers, Inquire about the root cause or concern, State diplomatic observations, and Mediate to resolution. *[Elaborate]*

Note: In this instance, an example was not needed because the elaboration provided the necessary context.

Following this simple three-step outline allows you to focus on exactly what the learner needs to know, no more and no less.

The Active Voice

Increasing the use of active voice is another technique to both avoid wordiness and add engagement and interest in your microlearning content. When you use the active voice the subject of the sentence performs the action with the verb; with the passive voice, the action is in the form of the helping verb *to be*. The active voice is more direct and easier to read than the passive voice. While you won't be able to use the active voice for every sentence, it does pay dividends to insert it when you can.

When reviewing your script, look for any form of the verb "to be"—such as *is, are, was, were, be,* or *been*—which may reveal the passive voice. For example, in the sentence "The expense form was completed on January 15," the subject (the expense form) is being acted upon (was completed); therefore, the sentence is passive. To make the sentence active, you need to identify the doer of the action; let's call him Juan. Now, the active voice sentence reads, "Juan completed the expense form on January 15."

When possible use active voice in microlearning scripts because it moves the written and spoken word to a more conversational tone, which studies have shown is better for learning. But be careful. E-learning researchers Ruth Clark and John Mayer (2011) point out that "you want to write with sufficient informality so that the learners feel they are interacting with a conversational partner but not so informally that the learner is distracted, or the material is undermined."

Questions

A great deal of microlearning creation centers on asking the learner to retrieve content from their memories. You can achieve this through questioning techniques. Because retrieving content is such an integral part of many microlearning designs, it's important to review some guidelines for creating good microlearning questions that trigger learning and help learners reduce the forgetting curve.

Make Questions Precise and Clear, Then Test Them

One of the first guidelines is to create questions that are precise and objective and avoid those that are ambiguous or subjective (Kapp 2003). An objective question is one in which multiple people scoring a test can all agree on the correct answer. This is important because when a question is seen as incorrect or there could be more than one answer, the focus tends to move to the design of the question and not the content you are trying to teach. Answers should be clear and not open to debate.

The next guideline encourages you to keep your questions at the appropriate reading and vocabulary level. You want the questions to test the knowledge of the employees, not their ability to read. Some environments like pharmaceutical sales can over-rely on scientific terms and concepts. However, you might also design microlearning for employees who speak English as a second language. In those situations, you need to be careful with your choice of wording and structure.

You can make sure your questions are clear and on the right reading level by testing them beforehand with a group of trainers or a small group of the intended audience. This will help ensure that your learners are not misinterpreting or confused by your questions. If you change any questions, adjust and retest. The focus should be on the content, not structure, of the question. This might take multiple rounds.

Measure Different Learning Depths

Next, include questions that measure a variety of depths of learning. Many questions will be related to the participant's memorization and ability to recall information. While these questions are important, they are not the only type that should be used for microlearning.

Consider using questions that force the learner to understand the content and its ramifications. An example is asking the learner about forward scheduling as part of project management. The learner understands that to forward schedule, they start with today's date and look forward into the future to determine when the work would be completed. They might not be able to apply the concepts, but they are able to comprehend what it means in addition to just memorizing the term.

Of course, once a person comprehends a concept, the next step is application. So if a person understands forward scheduling, can they actually do it? Testing this would involve giving the learner some data and question parameters and asking them to forward schedule. If they properly chose the date given the parameters of the question, they know how to forward schedule. You can use application questions to judge performance. They can play an important role in helping to change or reinforce behavior when they are used in a microlearning format.

The last type of question is an analysis question. This determines if the learner can analyze the situation and make judgements. Continuing with our example, you might give the learner a situation related to scheduling and then ask them whether forward or backward scheduling is better for that situation. In this case, the learner needs to read the situation, know the definition and application of forward and backward scheduling, know which is the most appropriate, and then make the choice. It requires much more cognitive processing but can help reinforce their understanding of the concepts.

As you can see, using questions to create microlearning content related to the testing effect can involve multiple levels of learning beyond simple memorization. If you craft the questions correctly, you can create a robust learning opportunity.

Podcasting

The great thing about podcasts or audio-only clips as a microlearning tool is that learners can listen when they are doing something else, like commuting to work or going for a jog. But like any piece of microlearning content, you need to keep the learner tuned in. This starts with focusing on the pace and presentation of the information. That is why it's critical to have a clear, concise, and compelling message. Its appeal comes from the delivery style of the presenter.

Here are some tips for creating an effective podcast. They cover where to record, what equipment is needed, what to do with your phone, how to open the podcast, and how to address the listener.

Find a comfortable and (this goes without saying) quiet place to record. If you are often or easily disturbed, you'll need to either record multiples times or spend a lot of time editing out the interruptions.

Once you know where to record, you want to make sure you have the right equipment. While you'll want a high-quality microphone or headset, the equipment doesn't have to be expensive. To decide between a mic and a headset consider whether you tend to move a lot when you speak. If you do, a headset might be better because your mic will stay with you if you move your head. With a stationary microphone, your volume will change if you move your head or don't maintain a consistent distance as you record.

Next, you might want to have a glass of room temperature water close by to help keep your mouth from becoming dry. Room temperature is best because a beverage that is too cold can "freeze" your vocal cords and a beverage that is too hot can burn if you unconsciously take a big swig. Consider avoiding carbonated beverages too. The last thing you want is to start hiccupping during recording or to have to edit out a burp or the constant fizzing of your drink. Finally, when you do take a drink, put the microphone on mute. Listening to someone swallow is not very engaging.

Using lip balm to moisturize your lips before podcasting will help reduce lip-smacking noises.

Turn off any nearby phones, whether they're landline or smartphone. This is an easy tip to forget! If you've got a landline phone, consider unplugging the cord so it doesn't ring suddenly. Turn your cellphone off; don't just set it to vibrate. Even a vibrating phone can be picked up with a sensitive microphone.

When you open the podcast, keep your introduction relatively short, maybe 20-30 seconds. Remember, people want to hear content and you don't have long to capture the learner, so hook them early. Try opening with some great content and then sneak in the title and other intro information later. But don't forget to tell the listeners your name. You wouldn't want to sit in a classroom not knowing the name of the instructor because they never introduced themselves; the same is true in a microlearning podcast.

When you are talking to the learners, refer to them as *you*. Think of the podcast as a conversation with the learner rather than a monologue. This way you can engage with them and they feel as if you are speaking to them personally. You might consider having a picture of an audience member handy to focus your attention on. Having something to "talk to" can help you feel less like you are talking to air and more like you are talking to real people.

Podcasts often require some post-production time and effort, since live recording rarely goes flawlessly. While in post-production, consider adding introduction music, ambient sounds, and an interview format to engage and keep the learners listening.

Graphic Layout and Aesthetics

You will see many types of graphics in microlearning, such as infographics and job aids, because they provide a concise presentation of content in a short format. When adding images to an infographic or to online content, remember, "there are times when pictures can aid learning, times when pictures do not aid learning but do no harm, and times when pictures do not aid learning and are distracting" (Reider 1994). Strive to have the images or graphics within your microlearning add value and not distract the learner.

Regardless of the graphic type, your goal is the same. You want to succinctly and effectively convey the right instructional message. (There's the K-I-S-S principle again.) Do not include graphics simply for the sake of adding visuals. Each graphic should have a purpose or outcome. For example, think about a CPR poster. Using icons and short actionable statements, the steps a person takes to administer CPR are laid out in a clean, easy-to-follow format. The imagery and short statements make the steps easier to recall, allowing the individual's reaction time to be minimized when administering CPR.

One method for identifying items to represent visually in a single, focused message is to look for content that is complex or confusing. Graphics can help add clarity to instructional content that is difficult to grasp with just text descriptions, and also help break it into smaller pieces. They provide a concise explanation of a topic and help organize the learner's thoughts and provide an anchor on which you can tether other concepts and ideas.

When selecting graphics, keep the learner's end goal in mind. Photographs, hyper-realistic images, or expertly rendered computer-generated images can provide a high level of detail, but they are most effective when the learner is experienced and precise application is required. For example, reading an echocardiogram of the heart requires looking at an actual photograph to have the highest degree of learning. However, that photograph might contain too much detail if you only want to teach the basic anatomy of the heart. In that case, a simple drawing might be more advantageous to learning than the detail of a photo-realistic image.

If you need to relate data or statistics to your learners, you may want to use charts or graphs to display the content. These can be powerful tools because they convey a great deal of meaning in a relatively small space, which is perfect for microlearning. With a well-designed chart, a quick glance will usually communicate the required information.

There are a few key pieces of information you should include in your graph or chart to help the learner quickly interpret the information. Don't underestimate the need for a descriptive and informative title. A well-titled chart will tell the learner what's being displayed and, possibly, the relationship of the data on the chart. Next, don't forget to include a key or legend, which functions as a translator, telling the learner what the different shades, colors, or patterns mean. The legend can even be embedded in the description of the graphic, as is often the case with infographics. Regardless of where it is located, the legend is necessary for the learner to understand what you are presenting.

If you decide to include a flowchart, make sure that you clearly explain what each symbol means and indicate which direction the information or inventory or whatever you are describing flows. Plus keep it simple. Since this is microlearning, it might make sense to show an entire, somewhat complex flowchart and then zoom in to the portion the program will explain.

Video

Since microlearning often features video content, here are some recommendations for creating compelling video-based microlearning pieces. This information is based on the research conducted by Philip Guo, an assistant professor of Computer Science at the University of Rochester, as well as our own experiences working on video-based courses. Guo's research is based on observations of more than 6.9

million instances of people watching edX videos (Guo, Kim, and Rubin 2014); we have experienced staring at LinkedIn Learning and other videos and conducted focus groups with learners to find out what makes the most sense in terms of delivering video-based content. What follows is our combined wisdom.

Don't ever, *ever* try to save time by simply recording an in-class lecture or workshop and then breaking that into smaller videos to pass off as microlearning. The classroom setting always creates a distance between the learner and the instructor and a video of a classroom creates an even greater distance. We know it's tempting because it's relatively easy and cheap and doesn't take a lot of planning, but this is not a good way to convey a learning message. Instead, you need to invest time upfront. We cover this in chapter 6 when we talk about pre-production. We have found that the more time you spend up front planning how the microlearning will unfold, the better it is from a production perspective and, more importantly, from the learner perspective.

Next, just having slides with a disembodied voice is not only ineffective from a learner perspective but it's downright painful to watch. We all know this! If at all possible, include video of the instructor every once in a while as the slides are presented. Better yet, think of it as a video of the instructor or trainer with interspersed slides, not the other way around. Also, use an enthusiastic trainer who speaks at a rate between 125 and 145 words per minute. This will keep the learners' attention. Enthusiasm is just as engaging in a video as it is in a classroom setting.

This next tip can probably be tied right back to reality TV. Learners no longer expect a production that is movie theatre quality.

Smartphones, quick video, and YouTube can create videos that feel more personal and connected. That connection and ability to directly talk to the learner is highly effective from a learning perspective. So, keep it informal. You can use smartphones or inexpensive cameras and still make an impact.

Think about the type of microlearning video you are creating and design it accordingly. For example, if you're creating a how-to video, you might want to place bookmarks or links so the learner can find exactly what they are looking for. For a lecture-based video, you can be reasonably certain the learner is only going to watch it once or twice, so you want to focus on that first, initial watching experience and not worry so much about whether the person is going to rewatch it. Spoiler alert: They probably won't.

"Explainer" or whiteboard microlearning video uses animation rather than a live person talking or a demonstration of a process. Here are a few tips to creating these successfully:

- **Don't use too many bells and whistles.** The software for creating explainer videos often contains many features and tools for special effects like fading in or out and camera movement. While they can be used effectively, if you pile one feature upon another, the learner will get caught up in the movement and special effects and lose track of the learning. Keep it straightforward and use special techniques sparingly.

- **Audio is important.** Make sure you have high-quality audio without background noises or the low audio hum caused by sub-par headsets or recording with the computer fan running in the background.

- **Consider using a story to deliver your instruction.** Stories can draw in the learner and provide the context for the instruction. They are highly effective in explainer videos.
- **Provide constant movement.** Remember your eyes process visuals quickly, so keep the learner engaged with different drawings and movement.

Gamification

Gamification means using game-based mechanics, aesthetics, and game thinking to engage people, motivate action, promote learning, and solve problems. It facilitates learning and encourages motivation through the use of game elements. Microlearning often uses what is referred to as *structural gamification,* which is the application of game elements to propel a learner through content with no alteration or changes to the content. For example, a learner receives 10 points for answering a question correctly; if they correctly answer enough questions, they might receive a badge. These two elements, combined with others, encourage the learner to interact with the content.

In gamification, the learners do not play an entire game from start to finish; rather they participate in activities that include elements from games, such as earning points, overcoming a challenge, or receiving badges for accomplishing a task. Game-based elements commonly seen in video or mobile games are integrated into the microlearning program to motivate the learners and keep them engaged with the content on a regular basis. Table 7-2 shows game elements align with desired outcomes.

If you'd like to know more about gamification, see Karl's book *The Gamification of Learning and Instruction.*

Table 7-2. Game Elements and Their Use

Game Element	Use
Points	• Level of correctness • Doing the right thing • Accomplishments over time
Progress (bar, game board)	• Accomplishments over time • Progress toward goal
Badge	• Gaining knowledge • Recognition of an accomplishment
Leaderboard	• Performance relative to others • Performance against standard or self • Sense of belonging and contributing
Avatar	• Accomplishments over time • Individuality • Recognition of accomplishment
Levels	• Gaining knowledge • Progress toward goal
Story	• Providing context and purpose
Socialization Aspects	• Sense of belonging and contributing • Sense of purpose

Short Sims

In addition to gamification, the short sim is another way to drive learner engagement with microlearning content. Clark Aldrich, international simulation designer, has pioneered the concept of short sims, which he defines as an interactive experience that takes a user between five and 15 minutes to finish. Aldrich states that short sims can introduce a topic, allow a learner to play with the concepts, and provide basic role plays and lab experiments. Instead of using a full-blown branching simulation to teach or reinforce a concept, the learner simply interacts with a character in the simulation, making realistic choices and receiving feedback on their input. The advantage is that while a full-blown simulation can take a long time to develop and deliver, a short sim can focus on one element and be created in a lot less time.

Figure 7-1 shows a screenshot from a short sim. In this sim, the learner only interacts with one character and only focuses on performing one task—getting past the gatekeeper. The player can engage with the sim as many times as they want, but the goal is always the same, get past the gatekeeper. Once the learner is successful, the sim is over. There are not multiple characters or multiple scenes. There is only one scene and one goal.

The short sim format keeps the learner focused, providing a quick way to practice and apply critical decision-making skills.

Figure 7-1. Example of a Short Sim

Image of a short sim created with LearnBrite software, showing a sales interaction between a sales rep and a hospital staff member.

Short sims can also present processes for learners to perform, remembering past decisions and previous sessions. They can even give diagnostic feedback or partial credit. Including a series of short sims in a microlearning curriculum can be highly effective, allowing learners to apply knowledge without having to spend hours in a full-blown, complex simulation.

When developing a short sim, it's important to keep the following in mind:

- **Short sims are about doing.** The learner has to do something, make a decision, take an action, or move an item from one place to another. If you can't assign a behavior or action to your content, don't create a short sim. Think action and activity, not content and memorization.

- **Always think about measuring success.** When you design a short sim, think about how you'll determine learner success. Did they made the right decisions, did they move the right object? The metrics can tell when a task is done poorly or expertly. Often an action or decision in a short sim is tied to a rubric, with each level in the rubric tied to a good, better, or best scoring system. This allows the learner to learn the difference between a good choice and the best choice.

- **Short sims are reality-based.** The short sim should be based on an actual situation the learner might encounter. It's is not a game. Short sims are often used as a social simulator, where some type of interaction between two or more people is evaluated. Or, it's the simulation of a piece of equipment or machinery.

Storyboarding

Now that we've given you the tips you need to create microlearning and described how to make it engaging, you'll want to actually build some microlearning. However, before you do that, we strongly suggest you create a storyboard for your microlearning development.

The storyboarding process ensures that you fully use the limited instructional time available in a microlearning lesson. Scripting out your microlearning using what we've included in this chapter and then combining it with the technology and level of engagement will provide the biggest impact for microlearning. Regardless of the technology you're using, you want a well laid-out plan for each microlearning product you create—from a script for video or podcasting to a rough sketch of an infographic.

Sketching artwork for an infographic or a poster seems relatively straightforward; you simply take out some paper or a computer art program and rough something up or drag and drop clipart to create the general idea. But it's important to do before you commit to paying an artist to interpret your vision.

If your microlearning program involves podcasts or video, storyboarding can become a little more involved. When storyboarding a video-based or animated microlearning event it helps to create a table that shows:

- what the instructor or SME will say or what will be displayed on the screen if there's no audio
- what the learner will see onscreen as they are watching the instructional content
- what digital assets will be used—for example, an image, a chart, a diagram, or a video or whiteboard drawing.

The idea is to give the developer creating the microlearning the information they need to create it, as well as make sure they know what assets they need to gather or create to add to the video production. For example, Table 7-3 shows that the animator or producer will need someone to create a whiteboard drawing for the second part of the script. It helps to know what needs to be created or what images need to be located prior to recording the microlearning.

Table 7-3 is a chart Karl used for a course on grant writing. It shows what is going to be said during the video, what files are needed for post-production, and which element goes with which part of the instruction.

Table 7-3. Storyboard for a Microlearning Lesson

Script	Blocking	Asset
One question frequently asked is, "How do I find a funding agency?" The question is straightforward but there are many ways to answer it. Fortunately, there are more resources available for finding funding sources than ever before.	Kapp Talking	Clip art file; File facultytalking.png
One good place to start is with seasoned colleagues. Ask at conferences or within your own institution where they have received funding or what big agencies or organizations fund initiatives within the field or specialty. If your field has a trade show with vendors, ask some of them if their organization provides any grant or funding opportunities.	Two faculty members talking to one another in the hall or at a conference.	Use hand drawing on whiteboard showing the following bullets: • Seasoned Colleagues • Conferences • Your Own Institution • Trade Show Vendors
Another great place to start looking for federal grants is Grants.gov. This is the place to find and apply for federal grants. You can search for United States federal grants with keywords or phrases; for example, let's say you wanted to find a grant related to "classroom technology." Simply enter the words into the search box and you will receive every grant that contains those keywords issued by the federal government.	Show website	Grants.gov (Show the search process for "Classroom Technology." Take approximately five steps. Record click through to show while person is talking.)
You can then drill down into the specific grant solicitation and see general information about the agency, due dates, eligibility criteria, and other key information.	Show drill down to a specific grant solicitation.	Grants.gov

This type of script can work for video-based microlearning or any other type of animated microlearning, such as a cartoon animation, stop-motion videos, or whiteboard explainer videos.

Short and Sweet

Designing microlearning is not unlike designing any other learning asset. It requires knowledge of the technology, an understanding of the learning goals, and some work to make it as effective as possible. Since the time is much shorter in microlearning than other learning programs, it's critical that the quality of the production meets the expectations of the learners.

Using the tips and techniques from this chapter will provide a good foundation for getting started. But keep in mind that this is just the tip of the iceberg—there are entire chapters, books, and courses on each of these topics. For example, Karl has several online courses related to gamification as well as three books on the topic. So, if you find yourself in need of a deep dive, it's in your best interest to find other resources to up your microlearning game.

Once you've planned the design of your microlearning product, it's time to follow up on measuring your effectiveness. We'll tackle that in the next chapter.

Key Takeaways

Based on the information from this chapter, the following conclusions can be drawn about designing microlearning:

- Writing Style
  - Keep it simple, short, and to the point, avoiding unnecessary words.

- Favor active rather than passive voice, which will help you use a conversational, informal tone.
- Remember three rules of conciseness: set it up, elaborate, and give an example (as needed).

- Questions
  - Create questions that are precise and objective. Test questions in advance to make sure they aren't subjective.
  - Keep the questions at the appropriate reading and vocabulary level for the audience.
  - Include questions that measure the different levels of learning: memorization, comprehension, application, and analysis.
- Podcasting
  - Find a comfortable and quiet place to create the podcast and use good equipment.
  - Jump into the content sooner rather than later. Provide some instruction and then do the introduction.
  - Add or subtract elements in post-production to make the podcast as engaging as possible.
- Graphics and Visuals
  - Make sure the graphics add value and don't distract the learner.
  - Do not include graphics simply for the sake of visuals. Each graphic should have a meaning, a purpose, and a message.
  - Identify content to be visualized by looking for areas of complexity or potential confusion.

- Video
  - Invest in pre-production lesson planning to create concise instructional scripts.
  - Intersperse an instructor's talking head with onscreen graphics and text.
  - Introduce motion and continuous visual flow into tutorials along with extemporaneous speaking.
  - Don't record a training session and then break it into microlearning segments.
- Gamification
  - Identify success criteria before you begin to gamify learning events.
  - Make scoring and winning transparent.
  - Use points to provide feedback on an answer's or activity's level of correctness.
  - Use badges to signal the participant has learned the content or mastered a subject.
  - Use leaderboards to show performance relative to others and progress toward goals.
- Short Sims
  - Keep the interactions limited so you don't confuse the learner.
  - Use sims to help learners gain a deeper understanding and build conviction, understand processes, and enjoy engaging with learning.

- Storyboarding
  - For infographics or posters, sketching or drawing by hand might be enough. You can also use software designed for quick prototyping.
  - If you are creating an animated or live video, use a three-column chart to help determine the flow.
  - Indicate what the audio will be, what visuals will appear (if any), and what digital assets are required.

8.
Measuring the Effectiveness of Microlearning

Chapter Questions

At the end of this chapter, you should be able to answer these questions:

- Why is it important to measure the effectiveness of microlearning?
- What opportunities for evaluation do microlearning provide?
- Can microlearning be evaluated by Kirkpatrick's four levels of evaluation?
- Who should you evaluate other than the learners when using microlearning?
- How can training developers evaluate the microlearning development process for workflow and sustainment purposes?

By now we hope we've stressed how creating and using microlearning does not mean disregarding learning and development best practices. While it's easy to focus on the design, development, and implementation stages, you should not neglect evaluation. Why spend all that effort only to come away not knowing its effectiveness? You want to know if your microlearning is changing performance and making a difference within the organization and with the learners.

Let's see how one organization is implementing microlearning and how it allows learners to track their progress. This case study, supplied by microlearning platform company Axonify, highlights this perfectly.

John Hancock's Use of a Dashboard to Evaluate Microlearning

Financial services is an increasingly complex world. Regulations are difficult to understand and constantly changing. At the same time, employees are required to possess a considerable wealth of knowledge about product portfolios and corporate policies. Keeping it all top of mind can be next to impossible, especially for new employees who are often firehosed with information during onboarding. While still important, a traditional training approach made up of infrequent classroom sessions, lunch-and-learns, and department meetings simply cannot meet the demands of a modern financial services workplace.

This is the reality John Hancock Investments faced in 2014 during a time of considerable change in their business. According to Charles A. Rizzo (2017), senior vice president and chief financial officer for the John Hancock Group of Funds, "When you have increased levels of complexity, the inherent risk is that people may not understand the policies and procedures well enough to provide a certain level of service that we're contracted to perform, or effectively control risk." Rizzo was looking for a way to help his team mitigate risk while also improving employee performance. Not only did he want information to move more quickly within the organization, but he also wanted to improve the consistency and retention of that information. "People should get just what they need when they need it to perform at their best," he explained.

Although Rizzo's background is in finance, not learning and development, he stumbled on a possible way to address his problem while reading *Exponential Organizations* by Salim Ismail. The book referenced Axonify, a learning technology company in Waterloo, Ontario, which was applying microlearning to solve similar business problems. The concept of microlearning was a new one for Rizzo, but within a few months he was introducing it through Axonify within his own team at John Hancock.

Since implementing microlearning in 2014, John Hancock has realized clear business value from its new learning strategy. "After we rolled out Axonify to more than 100 employees, we saw a direct correlation between participation rates, employee engagement, and performance," Rizzo explained. "Our folks are increasingly understanding the roles and responsibilities of other groups within our department." Most importantly, employees who engage consistently in microlearning made fewer errors.

John Hancock uses Axonify to deliver microlearning sessions to financial services employees in less than five minutes per day. Each session leverages the learning science principle of retrieval practice by asking three to five questions focused on high-priority information for the employee's specific role. Questions are repeated at varying intervals over multiple sessions to make sure employees retain the information over time. They start with foundational information on products and processes and then, as their knowledge grows over weeks to months, they answer more application and scenario-based questions.

The microlearning sessions are completed on the employees' work computers or mobile devices.

John Hancock leverages motivational tactics to make the microlearning experience more fun and engaging. Employees have the option to play a simple game as part of each session. They also receive points by completing their training and answering questions correctly, which places them on a competitive leaderboard with their teammates. These tactics, along with the high-quality, job-specific content, have helped drive microlearning participation north of 90 percent, with employees completing an average of 15 sessions a month.

Microlearning also provides more timely, actionable data than the organization had ever gathered through traditional training practices. Using dashboards with real-time data visualizations, managers can quickly see who is and is not participating in training. They can dig into an employee's profile to determine specific areas of need to provide individualized coaching and identify areas of expertise. Senior management can gauge the organization's current level of knowledge on critical topics at a glance, without having to build complex spreadsheets or pivot tables.

John Hancock has been leveraging microlearning principles for five years as a key component of its learning transformation efforts. In just five minutes per day, it makes sure its employees retain and apply the critical knowledge they need to do their jobs effectively, avoid risk, and deliver high-quality service to their customers. And it's all grounded in evidence-based learning science principles and modern technology. From Rizzo's standpoint, "the key value add of microlearning is we are able to push out content that is critical to our business while providing consistent information to every member of our team. Microlearning makes it easier to refresh content continuously to fit the evolving nature of our business, the changing complexity of our products, and the different services that we perform."

Why Measurement and Evaluation Matters

As you can see, the John Hancock organization was able to make real-time measurements on the effectiveness of the microlearning through dashboards and other reporting tools built into the platform. This provides timely and actionable information related to the effectiveness of the learning happening within the organization.

We wish that this type of actionable, easily available data is the norm in the industry, but from what we've seen and experienced, it isn't. We've seen plenty of disappointment and frustration because a full evaluation plan wasn't considered as part of the learning initiative. Disregarding an evaluation plan at the outset may mean you won't know what went wrong if something did—or why something went right, so you can do it again. Was your content on the mark, but learners couldn't access it because you didn't share it? Or was your content not helpful even though learners could view it?

It might not seem like a big deal to cut corners and ignore the evaluation efforts needed to determine the effectiveness of your training. But evaluation is the only way you'll be able to tell how effective or worthwhile your efforts were. We know it's a bummer when your ideas and efforts were solid but the execution failed somewhere along the way and your training team or your learners, or both, suffer.

We don't think you've been hiding under a rock, so we'll assume you're aware that data is becoming more of a must for improving performance and developing talent within organizations. Granted, data has always been essential, but the demand has grown, especially because of the push to focus on learning performance (not to mention shrinking training budgets). That's why we signaled the importance of measurement and evaluation from the start in chapter 3, when we listed possible measures alongside design considerations and contextualized examples in our use cases.

We also know that there are folks that jump on the innovation bandwagon only to get burned. Our experience has taught us that this failure largely happens when a stakeholder demands the new "it" thing without ensuring you have the capacity to manage, scale, and sustain it, let alone evaluate it. This short-sighted thinking about performance development has increased with microlearning due to the notion that mobile technology and a culture of "need it now, know it now" creates a "build it and they will use it" mentality that isn't substantiated. Then add the idea that people think the performance or behavior will change rapidly (or even instantly) because it was delivered using new techniques and technology! Again, not true.

If you want to keep afloat, you will have to look at the evaluative opportunities of microlearning and whether they lead to learning, behavior change, performance improvement, and ultimately results. But also don't forget to evaluate your development efforts, which will help set you up for continued success!

The First Step

To begin your evaluation efforts, you need a thorough plan for how you'll design the process, collect the data, and report the results. You start this process by asking the key questions of who, what, why, when, where, and how you'll evaluate. These questions are similar to those we offered in chapter 3 to help sort out how to address a use case. Let's use an example as we go through the question: A compliance department with a key performance indicator for reducing compliance-related issues for the entire organization. In this scenario, ask:

- **Who?** Who are you evaluating? Just the learners? The learners and their managers? The learners and the instructor? Customers?
- **What?** What are you specifically going to know about? What topics or behaviors? Which compliance-related issues? Your microlearning asset will not cover every topic on compliance, only the ones that help achieve the reduction you desire. Perhaps all topics were related to reporting compliance. In that case you want to know: Who should report, why it's their responsibility to report, what is reportable, when to report, and how to report.
- **Why?** Why are you evaluating the people you identified? What are you hoping to know, learn, confirm, and so on? The "why" is your intended or desired outcome. In our example, the learning initiatives were done for compliance department employees and for all employees based on job roles and position. Here you have different answers to gain from the why. Reporting is not only everyone's responsibility (employees), but it's also the compliance department's responsibility to know which ones are valid and which to report.
- **When?** When is the best time to gather information for what you want to know? Sometimes it is immediately, because you don't want to lose the learner's authentic reaction, thoughts, and opinions. However, there are times when holding off is more important for determining if the result has been achieved. For example, you would want to test the learners

on their compliance-reporting knowledge at time of training. But, measuring whether the training improved the compliance-related issue will need to be done over time and probably not just once. Here you may opt to look at data in three-, six-, nine-, and 12-month intervals.

- **Where?** What locations make an ideal spot for gathering data? Perhaps observation on the production floor, a paper form, or an online survey. What will help to promote gathering the data and not hinder its collection?

- **How?** How are you going to collect this information? This is the literal action or tool that will gather the necessary feedback you need. You may use more than one action or tool as well. For example, you may use quarterly reports on compliance to gather some data, in addition to sending a quick survey to all training participants on whether they reported a compliance issue (or issues) that quarter.

Answering these questions provides an effective process for conducting the evaluation. The one missing element is an actual evaluation model. You need a way to think about measuring the effectiveness of the microlearning itself. We suggest using a well-known model in the field: Kirkpatrick's four levels of evaluation, which was actually conceived by Raymond Katzell in the 1950s but popularized by Donald Kirkpatrick.

The Power of Kirkpatrick

While it has come under fire lately, the Kirkpatrick model of evaluation (influenced strongly by the work of Kratzell) has helped transform industry thinking about evaluation. The Kirkpatrick-Katzell four levels of evaluation model helps measure the effectiveness of learning products. Don Kirkpatrick, and then his son Jim and daughter-in-law Wendy, have used this framework to set many training and development professionals on a solid evaluative path for decades.

The first level of evaluation features self-reported data from the learners, and the model expands on that reporting up to the fourth level, which focuses on the return of the training initiative toward departmental or organization outcomes. Table 8-1 is a quick look at the four levels.

Now let's combine our evaluation plan questions with the Kirkpatrick-Katzell evaluation model to see how an effective evaluation plan can be put into action (Table 8-2).

Notice the worksheet begins with the identification of what is being evaluated. This might seem like common sense, but often an evaluation plan is thrown off because people have different expectations of what is being evaluated. Having it in writing ensures that everyone is focused on evaluating the same element. Also notice that we aren't evaluating the training itself, we are evaluating the outcome of the training, which is the accuracy of the reports. Measuring the effectiveness of microlearning means measuring outcomes that matter to the business.

Next, the worksheet indicates why the evaluation is being undertaken. The purpose is to determine why the reports are not accurate, why issues are unreported, and why leadership and managers are not always able to comprehend how to help with compliance issues. The why indicates the exact problem or problem set the training is intended to solve. Again, this keeps the evaluation in scope. There may be many problems related to compliance, but this evaluation plan is only looking to solve one.

Table 8-1. Quick Overview of the Kirkpatrick-Katzell Four Levels of Evaluation

Level of Evaluation	Description	Examples
1 Reaction	What does the learner think about the training immediately upon taking or participating in it? Input can range from how appealing the learner found the content to the pace to whether the learner thought they learned something to whether the learner thought the material was easy to understand.	• Post-workshop survey • Rating on a help page (how helpful was this article) • Focus group discussions
2 Learning	Did the learner pass the test and demonstrate knowledge acquisition? This evaluation level occurs as part of the overall learning initiative, whether at the end of all information being presented or throughout. This is where assessments ascertain if the learning objectives were actually met by the audience.	• Multiple choice, true/false, fill-in-the blank, essay-style exams • Rubrics (e.g., when evaluating a presentation, sales calls, or handling conflict in a team setting) • Simulations (e.g., land plane on water)
3 Behavior	Is there evidence of the learned content in the workflow or work performance? After a learner passes the test, this evaluation level measures whether they are actually using the information in practice. This can occur within days, a few weeks out, or even months later.	• Survey to the learners (more in depth than Level 1; these questions help gauge the amount of knowledge or skill being recalled and/or applied to job tasks) • Survey to the learners' managers • Review of job performances • Visual observation
4 Results	Is there evidence that the initiative is closing the gap on the known issue? Like a gauntlet, this is the largest hurdle to get across. This level means proving that the learning program is affecting the bottom line.	• Baseline data on the issue compared with post-learning initiative data • Performance of the individual (annual performance review) • Other markers your organization has identified as success indicators

Table 8-2. The Kirkpatrick-Katzell Model in Action

What is being evaluated?	The type, accuracy, and quantity of compliance reports submitted
Why is it being evaluated?	• Several issues have gone unreported, creating operational issues for the organization. • Reports are also lacking in essential details that assist the compliance department in making determinations on whether or not to report. • Managers and leadership do not always know how to assist employees with compliance-based issues.

Level	Who?	Where?	When?	How Will You Evaluate?
1 Reaction	Learner	Online	Right after each piece of microlearning is provided	• Survey, using a star-rating system
2 Learning	Learner	Online	During each lesson (self-check) and at the end (mastery)	• Video-based scenarios with multiple choice questions • Role play to complete a report given a circumstance • True/false and multiple choice on basic compliance concepts
3 Behavior	Learner	Online	1 month and 3 months after taking microlearning topic	• Survey using yes/no, Likert, and open-ended inquiry questions • A few assessment questions on the main objectives of the topic
	Manager	Online	1 month and 3 months after employees took the microlearning topic	• Survey using yes/no, data entry, and open-ended inquiry questions • An upload option for reports that were submitted that quarter • A few assessment questions on the main objectives of the topic
4 ROI	Manager	Online	6 months and 12 months after the last microlearning program was deployed	• Similar survey to the one provided in Level 3, but with additional data entry points for cumulative data

Then each level of the evaluation model is highlighted in the worksheet with specific elements, such as who is being evaluated and where. This can be critical because line managers may not want to take employees off "money-making tasks" to participate in training evaluation. If you can show that much of the evaluation will occur online or provide a specific timeframe for when employees will be offline, managers may be more likely to allow them to participate in the evaluation. The timeframe will also highlight that evaluation is a long-term process. Emphasize that you want to measure the effectiveness over time and not just once.

As you build information over time, you are setting baselines and gaining markers of change at different points. Establishing a long-term measurement of effectiveness may help the organization recognize that performance may waffle at different times during a year due to a myriad of reasons. Some may be as basic as end-of-year project completion to as big as a business merger or something in between, like a new VP in charge of your division. It's good to gain insights into those potential causes of performance change.

The final column indicates how you are going to conduct the evaluation. This helps to inform all stakeholders of the actions you will take to measure the microlearning and will help to get everyone on board. For example, if a survey method is not acceptable to the line manager or upper management, it's far better to know that now, in the planning stage, then when you go to try to administer the survey. We've seen training departments be severely reprimanded because they administered a survey without a VP's approval, not realizing that the organization was "surveyed out" and did not want any more surveys. Evaluation plans that are socialized within the organization ahead of time avoid those potential disasters.

Use this type of worksheet to plan your evaluation effort. Also, you don't need to use the Kirkpatrick-Kazwell model; there are many other evaluation models such as Will Thalheimer's Learning-Transfer Evaluation Model, Kaufman's Five Levels of Evaluation, and Jack and Patti Phillips's ROI Methodology.

Evaluating the Effort

With so much focus on evaluating whether your microlearning asset led to learning, behavior, or performance improvements, it's easy to lose sight of evaluating whether your development process was effective. Can you use the same approach to evaluate the learner and learning effectiveness for development effectiveness? Yes and no. You could use it to plan out how to gather information from specific audiences that helped get the training developed and implemented. However, that may be too tedious and detail-oriented, and it's definitely not somewhere we want to go with this chapter.

That's okay. Let's try a method that shares commonalities with the Kirkpatrick-Kazwell evaluation model: a SWOT analysis. You may be wondering how the strengths, weaknesses, opportunities, and threats (SWOT) provide an evaluative picture on your development process. First, it's going to help you quickly identify, from the experiences of the project, what was successful (strengths), what wasn't (weaknesses), what should be incorporated (opportunities), and what should be removed (threats).

When we talk about evaluative factors of training development entities, we focus largely on asking, "How can I do this as efficiently as possible, while still being effective?" You and your stakeholders might want to know about other evaluative factors, but most insights will stem from this key question. Notice we are not associating training effectiveness to training development efficiencies at this point. They are not technically interrelated. Yes, training can be less than effective because it was released late, perhaps because the training team was understaffed. However, that's not an issue of efficiency, that's a resourcing problem.

If you deployed the microlearning ineffectively because you did not understand how to distribute microlearning within the structure of the organization—that's an efficiency issue. But remember, if you discover that the training was ineffective, that does not mean it was due wholly to being inefficient. Sound instructional design principles still apply. Bottom line, it's going to be rare that the training team's development process prevents the microlearning from meeting its target outcomes with the target audience. Effectiveness is more likely influenced by the design of instruction.

Let's use a SWOT analysis to look at the training team that supported the development of compliance reporting microlearning series. Start by asking these questions:

- **Strengths.** What were your team's strongest capabilities in completing the initiative?
- **Weaknesses.** What were your team's vulnerable points in completing the initiative?
- **Opportunities.** What internal organizational advantages were not used in completing the initiative?
- **Threats.** What external factors, if any, could compromise the initiative or future ones like it?

With your answers, your analysis might look something like Figure 8-3.

Figure 8-3. SWOT Evaluation Analysis

Strengths
- Experienced staff were familiar with content
- SMEs were readily available
- Training staff was experienced with authoring tools and delivery system

Weakness
- First time producing microlearning
- Short timeframe to develop
- Small budget for development of materials
- Lack of coordination on marketing and distribution to all employees

Opportunities
- Develop a microlearning map
- Use same style guides that are in place for all learning development
- Use of data from initial project, (e.g., hours spent in redesigning training)

Threats
- Only Level 1 evaluation executed
- Stakeholders not fully vested in microlearning approach
- Training team only maintains training based on annual cycles and onboarding
- Annual retreat created a large demand on various resources associated with the project

Granted this might not be exhaustive, but it does a good job of demonstrating how to correlate the development and implementation of the initiative to the respective categories in the SWOT. Now that you've mapped out the information on the SWOT analysis, you want to examine it and locate areas where you could improve. From reviewing Figure 8-3, you will notice, without taking a deeper dive, some areas that will improve efficiency immediately:

- creating a microlearning strategy (opportunity)
- using currently approved styles and templates (opportunity)
- developing a marketing and distribution timeline that covers the roles of the learners and leadership (weakness).

There are also areas that are not as immediate, but you could dive into and solidify:

- determining data points and where and how to collect them for baselines (opportunity)
- developing an evaluation plan that can address the true intended outcome of the initiative (threat)
- modifying the maintenance cycle of the training products (threat).

Take a look at all the opportunities for improvement and begin prioritizing which opportunities can be addressed given your budget and capacity. In our example, having the organization begin to use approved styles and templates might be a relatively easy and quick fix, whereas modifying the maintenance cycle of training product might take a great deal of effort. The SWOT analysis should spur a prioritization exercise to determine what actions to take next. We've also seen training and development organizations use this type of approach at the end-of-year evaluation to determine design and development strategies and initiatives for the following fiscal year and for budgeting purposes.

Four Factors for Evaluation

Now, it's possible that the SWOT approach won't fit with your organization's thinking about evaluation development effectiveness. An alternate approach would be to go for a basic method that addresses four key efficiency factors: cost, resources, processes, and sustainment.

- **Cost.** Cost to create the piece and the overhead cost of the staff and equipment to create and maintain it.
  - Was the cost of the project similar to other projects?

- Were there unanticipated costs that had to be addressed for the project to be completed?
- **Resources.** People, equipment, content, and so on.
  - Were the people capable and experienced enough to create the microlearning?
  - Was the equipment satisfactory for development? Deployment?
  - Did the content need to be rewritten? Created from scratch?
  - Was there an expert to rely on for content verification?
- **Processes.** Internal to training team, departmental as related to training, working across departments, procuring resources, gaining approvals, and so on.
  - Did the team have to deviate from normal training development procedures?
  - Were new processes introduced by working with new departments or same departments, but with a different type of need (such as marketing)?
  - Were new processes identified that would have made the initiative run more smoothly?
- **Sustainment.** Infrastructure, resources, cost, and so on.
  - Does the organization have an established infrastructure that can sustain the current microlearning solution?
  - Does the training development team have an infrastructure in place that can support sustaining the microlearning solution?
  - Were there unidentified costs associated with sustaining the solution?

    ◦ Was an evaluation plan developed into the sustainment of
      the solution?

No matter the approach, it's important to look at new initiatives, and even ones already in operation, with an evaluative lens. You may discover that you are performing work optimally or you may find that you are not maximizing resources. Your team may find out that they can develop microlearning faster than a more traditional piece of training. Other notable factors that we have seen bubble out of these evaluations include:

- Data you've gathered during your evaluation of the microlearning that does not actually address outcomes.
- The new approach needs more introduction and lead time with the key individuals affected by the training. Why is the new approach being used? How will it affect my employees? Does it take away from their daily tasks?
- There was an expectation within the organization that performance improvement would be immediate.
- The budget did not factor for more overhead, enough staff, or equipment, which meant that the effort was underfunded and unable to meet expectations.
- The strategic fit of the initiative was misaligned.

Short and Sweet

Measuring the effectiveness of your microlearning effort is important. Not only should you want to know the outcomes of your efforts, but proof or evidence of learning outcomes is being increasingly demanded by upper management. Unfortunately, measuring the effectiveness of a learning effort is not trivial. You need to have an evaluation plan and then measure against that plan. In this chapter we covered how to go about creating your evaluation plan for microlearning. We talked about the need to know the who, what, where, when, and how, and we discussed the need to have an evaluation model to guide the process. Combining those two elements will provide you with a solid basis for determining how your microlearning efforts are affecting the organization.

Additionally, we discussed the need to evaluate your internal design efforts. Without self-reflection, your efforts may drift off course or become ineffective. It never hurts, even with seemingly impossible schedules, to take the time to see how you are performing. Following the steps outlined in this chapter provides you with framework against which you can measure your own effectiveness in developing microlearning.

Key Takeaways

Based on the information from this chapter, evaluation is multifaceted and necessary for determining effectiveness, sustainability, and feasibility:

- Kirkpatrick's four levels of evaluation is an easy way to map and plan how to gather information from the learners and about the learners.
- Microlearning provides opportunities to evaluate performance and behavior over time.
- Although it's valuable to evaluate the learners, it's also critical to evaluate those who supervise or manage the learners. It's also important to evaluate the processes that designed the microlearning or trained instructors for efficiency and capabilities.
- Two methods that training organizations can use to evaluate their development efforts are a SWOT analysis or an evaluation of cost, resources, processes, and sustainment.

Conclusion

As We Conclude, Ask Yourself

- What are the big takeaways, and what should we think about as we embark on creating microlearning?
- Why should you consider microlearning as part of your instructional toolkit?
- What is the future of microlearning?

Microlearning is simultaneously old and new. The concept of providing short, highly meaningful bits of instruction has been around for centuries. What's new is the ability to deliver training to an employee or student's smartphone via wireless or cellular technology. The need for using sound instructional design techniques isn't gone—it's still required.

Even though microlearning is shorter than other instructional initiatives, the best examples of microlearning still use time-tested instructional design methodologies. Just because we've changed how we access content in the past few years doesn't mean we have changed the fundamental nature of how we learn. No matter how we acquire information, we learn the same way our grandparents and their grandparents learned.

So, anyone who aspires to design microlearning needs to understand the new elements that give it its timely appeal—the easy-to-deliver and easy-to-create tools. Not to mention incorporating hundreds of years of research on how people learn, which supports placing microlearning into the process. Blissfully developing microlearning without understanding basics of instructional design is a dangerous path.

Let's see how one company has put together many facets of microlearning to help their organization.

Payoneer's Microlearning Implementation

Payoneer's mission is to "Empower businesses to go beyond—beyond borders, limits, and expectations." The company's platform streamlines global commerce for millions of small businesses, marketplaces, and enterprises from 200 countries and territories. Leveraging its technology, compliance, and banking infrastructure, Payoneer delivers a suite of services that includes cross-border payments, working capital, tax solutions, and risk management. Payoneer makes global commerce easy and secure by powering growth for customers ranging from entrepreneurs in emerging markets to the world's leading digital brands like Airbnb, Amazon, Google, and Upwork.

The business challenge for Payoneer, and what led them to microlearning, is that they operate in a highly regulated market. This means the company's more than 350 customer care associates around the world must be aware of and in compliance with hundreds of continuously changing regulations. For example, let's say a local central bank has revised its regulations and now requires that all money transfers include a signed statement from the client. Customer care associates must not only know this, they must remember it for relevant transfers and act accordingly, otherwise they may put themselves and the client at legal risk. Addressing this type of challenge in a fast-growing company that contains a multitude of different financial services in a complex global economy could prove to be difficult.

Initially, Payoneer's customer care department used daily face-to-face briefings to relay important updates to its customer care agents. Managers held these briefings at the beginning of each shift to train and inform agents on updates to procedures, services, laws, and regulations. However, as Payoneer's customer care department grew from a one-office operation to a global team operating around the clock to offer 24/7 support, this approach was no longer sustainable.

To address these constraints, Payoneer implemented a microlearning solution. The company had several design considerations. Its microlearning system needed to allow training content to be created easily and quickly. It also needed to offer templates and enable adapting and reusing existing content to quickly release updates, as well as the ability to easily localize content for different global units. Administrators also needed the ability to trigger specific content to different users at different times and create cadences based on their profile to ensure knowledge was relevant for all agents.

While Payoneer already had an LMS, its functionalities were designed more for long-form courses, record keeping, and certification, so could not easily be applied to meet this need.

Another major consideration was motivation. Payoneers' customer care associates are predominantly younger and accustomed to rapid feedback and highly engaging content formats. Without a mechanism for engagement, the L&D team was worried that daily training sessions would easily become a chore, with the focus being more on getting them done than on actual learning and retention. This could lead to delayed completion and lower than desired success rates in the post-session quizzes. Payoneer decided gamification would help resolve this engagement issue.

So, the L&D team decided on a two-pronged approach: daily microlearning bursts and a gamified microlearning platform. To create the microlearning bursts, the L&D team collected information and updates from different departments (including legal, product, and credit compliance). That information, which was typically a few paragraphs of text explaining the regulatory update and its implications, was followed by retrieval practice (a short quiz) to help ensure associates not only clicked through the content but assimilated and retained the knowledge. Payoneer disseminates these daily microlearning modules to all its associates worldwide.

The company worked with a platform vendor called Gameffective, which enables gamified microlearning and performance tracking. (An organization could do a similar approach in house, however, working with vendors is beneficial because they have experience implementing across a wide range of companies and cultures and can help make the microlearning program a success.)

Through the Gameffective platform, associates receive instant feedback and recognition in the form of points and badges for completing learning assignments and success on post-learning assessments. Each associate's dashboard is designed with a race car theme—by tracking their car on the race track, associates can track their progress as they complete their learning assignments.

Associates also pass levels and gain badges, creating social status and indicating level of mastery. These activities led to increased learner satisfaction scores and overall engagement with the program. Payoneer plans to further increase engagement by displaying race progression and leaderboards on TV screens in the company's common areas and offering redeemable prizes to employees in exchange for game points.

But Payoneer also wanted managers and leaders to have control and insights into the microlearning process. So, team managers and leaders were given access to a dashboard with reporting tools allowing them to track their reports' real-time completion, knowledge, and performance levels. Based on these, team leaders can follow up with employees to offer relevant coaching, and managers can easily see how well a certain learning item was understood and applied. All this enables continuous optimization of learning items and staying on top of potential future compliance issues.

The results help to drive success. Almost from the beginning, Payoneer reaped benefits from this combination of a microlearning and gamification approach. The company is now able to deliver more updates, faster and better than ever. In addition, the development and deployment time for new learning content has been cut by more than half. Whereas before, designing learning content and disseminating updates required hours of work across different modules, working within the microlearning and gamification platform enables the completion of much of this work in a matter of minutes.

Additionally, Payoneer has seen substantial improvement in the associates' post-learning assessment scores and compliance with training requirements. Employees are 9 percent more likely to log into the system and complete their learning daily, and their success rate has improved by 8 percentage points (from 82 percent to 90 percent). It should be noted that mandatory training is responsible for the high initial completion and success rates. This means that an already high participation and success rate was pushed even higher.

This impact is not only seen in immediate post-learning assessments—it is long lasting. Payoneers' L&D team conducts quarterly QA assessments to review knowledge levels of the topics covered throughout the quarter. It has seen a substantial improvement in the results of these assessments following the deployment of the program.

Lastly, and perhaps most importantly, employees are reporting a much higher satisfaction level from the L&D department and from the new learning approach. Overall satisfaction with the learning system has increased by 16 percent. Associates are not only more successful in their learning, they are more engaged and attentive, which leads to higher overall engagement and desire to succeed.

As a result of the success of the microlearning and gamification implementation, Payoneer's Neomie Rothnie, development and QA manager for customer care, has indicated that "We are already expanding this approach to more units of our organization, and are looking to integrate other gamification functionalities to strengthen our employees' motivation and engagement to the learning process." There can't be a better endorsement for microlearning than that.

Practical Considerations

The Payoneer case study shows how implementing the concepts in this book can make your microlearning a success. We've tried to supply just enough information here in *Microlearning: Short and Sweet* to provide you with the fundamentals to get started successfully.

We've defined microlearning and highlighted that it's not bounded artificially by a timeframe. But we've also told you that five to six minutes is a good timeframe for a microlearning video based on available research.

Throughout, we've strived for both a theoretical and real-world approach. It's great to academically define microlearning as unrestricted by time and instead focus on the learning outcome, but when you've rolled up your sleeves and your manager wants to know you'll have the microlearning curriculum done by Monday, a little guidance on the right length of time can be helpful and practical.

Pure researchers might say, "Well, it's inconclusive. We don't know if it's 4.5 minutes, 4.8 minutes, or even 3.25." No, we don't know that, but we do know that if the microlearning is not developed and deployed, it doesn't matter, so we've presented guidelines to help you make an informed decision. Use all the information in this book to make the right decisions for your microlearning implementation.

Microlearning Defined

A helpful approach we believe works well with determining the use of microlearning is using a framework that classifies and distinguishes the different use types. In this book we've created a framework of six use types of microlearning. Use this framework to think about how microlearning can be helpful for your situation and also to give your team a common language to talk about microlearning. It's important enough to repeat here:

- **Pensive microlearning.** Use this type of instruction to ask the learner to reflect upon an idea, situation, or learning task. The goal is to have the learner think through or brainstorm ideas or concepts through reflective inquiry.
- **Performance-based microlearning.** Use this type of instruction to assist the learner in performing a task in the

moment. It's also known as just-in-time or at point of need learning. If you've ever used a step-by-step how-to video to perform a household chore, you've used performance-based microlearning.

- **Persuasive microlearning.** Use this type of instruction to modify the learner's behavior. It gently reminds the learner of goals and prompts behaviorally focused actions. This type of microlearning is often used in exercise or wellness applications.

- **Post-instruction microlearning.** Use this type of instruction as a targeted follow up to a larger instructional event, such as a workshop or conference. It provides reminders and quizzes related to the key concepts from the larger training.

- **Practice-based microlearning.** Use this type of instruction as both a reminder to practice and a coach to help hone a skill. A good example of this is a language app on your phone—you receive reminders, tips, and practice opportunities all designed to help you speak a foreign language.

- **Preparatory/preparation or primary microlearning.** Use this type of instruction to set up a series of planned learning initiatives to prepare for a larger learning event such as a webinar or an all-day class session. This could be a refresher of content or it could be new, general content.

Theoretical Underpinnings for Microlearning

Sound instructional design is critical for successfully deploying microlearning in any type of learning environment, from governmental to nonprofit to academic to corporate. You need to use the following for success:

- **Learning theories** are paradigms that provide perspective on how learning is acquired, retained, and recalled. To that end, we provided a little information (microlearning) on the theories of behaviorism, cognitivism, constructivism, and connectivism.
- **Learning domains** comprise the knowledge, skills, and behaviors we attain. We provided a high-level overview and, hopefully, a refresher on the cognitive, affective, and psychomotor learning domains.

Having a grounding in the fundamentals of how and what we learn provides a helpful approach to designing your microlearning. You don't need to apply each aspect every time, and you don't even need to classify your microlearning as one theory or domain over another, but it is helpful to understand that different approaches are viable from an instructional perspective.

Eventually the domains and theories will surface unconsciously while you develop your microlearning and, we hope, any learning that you develop. Again, microlearning is not a mad departure from other types of learning, it's simply one of many approaches.

Empirical Studies As a Basis for Microlearning

Once learning theori are in place, the next step in advancing science is to conduct studies. Fortunately, the elements of microlearning have been investigated in hundreds of studies over, literally, hundreds of years. From the early work of Ebbinghaus and his examination of the forgetting curve to the studies on the spacing effect and the test effect, the research is clear about the value of these techniques to enhance recall and even change behaviors.

While we certainly don't have the last word from a research perspective on microlearning, it is evident that microlearning can be a powerful force for helping the modern learner. Our role as the designers of instruction is to leverage what we've learned here and combine it with what works with our own corporate culture and our own delivery methods.

We also can't rest on the existing research and ignore any new research. Part of our commitment to being professionals means that we must continually seek new studies and new research on microlearning. It's hard to keep up with sometimes, but the science of learning, or any science for that matter, doesn't remain static. We will have new insights and new directions in microlearning as it continues to be studied and examined.

What's Your Microlearning Strategy?

Microlearning, really any type of organized learning, needs to be grounded by the organization's strategy for helping its members. They might be employees or volunteers or even paying customers who want to learn a new language. Regardless, there needs to be a strategy for incorporating microlearning into the learning stream of the organization.

We spent a small chunk of the book describing considerations for a strategy from motivation to technology to formal and informal learning. As with any endeavor, you'll need to create a strategy and develop a plan. That doesn't mean things won't change or vary, but it does mean that you are prepared for changes and that you recognize the changes when they occur.

We've provided information on planning and implementing microlearning ranging from the factors that should be considered to how to think about risk and mitigating potential problems. The goal is to help you think through the microlearning process before you decide to just jump in. There are arguments for using it in an emergency or for short-term initiatives, but without an overall strategy and implementation plan the microlearning risks becoming "just another thing to do" on the learner's already full plate (and the training developers' too).

Creating Microlearning

The key to microlearning is brevity. As we mentioned earlier, when Karl was younger his grandmother would often start off her letter with a statement like, "Karl, I don't have time to write you a short letter, so this letter will be rather long." At the time, Karl had no idea what that meant. Wouldn't it take longer to write a longer letter?

Well, as Karl has gotten older, he's discovered that brevity is not synonymous with quickness. In fact, to create a concise, well-conceived message often takes much longer than writing a long, rambling one. If you are going to create truly effective microlearning, you've got to keep it simple, straightforward, and laser-focused on the instructional outcome you expect.

In chapter 7 we discussed ways to make your writing short and simple, and we dabbled in some production concepts for your microlearning. For each of those topics there are dozens and dozens of books. While we didn't take a comprehensive dive into those topics, we provided a starting point and enough information so if that was all you read on the subject (which we don't recommend) you could do a decent job with your microlearning creation.

Once you've used the guidelines and production techniques to get you off and running and hopefully creating a few microlearning pieces, seek out the gaps that exist in your creation process and close them.

To continually create effective microlearning, you'll need to continually learn new tools and techniques. The technology and methodologies aren't standing still, and neither should you.

Evaluating Microlearning

In today's data-driven society, there is no point in ignoring evaluation. If you are creating instruction of any kind, you want to know if it works. Microlearning is no exception. Now that doesn't mean every single microlearning program you create needs to be evaluated, but you do need to evaluate enough of your microlearning offerings to ensure that they are, in fact, providing the desired outcomes.

The evaluation needs to be at a high level, "Is the overall strategy working?" and at the individual asset level, "Does this microlearning piece actually teach what we need it to teach? Are learners learning?" The time to think about evaluation is before you launch a learning initiative and not after. Take time, as we explain in chapter 8, to look over your learning goals and create an evaluation plan. You want to know the results of your efforts so you can change, modify, or brag appropriately about the microlearning that's been created.

Future of Microlearning

No conclusion or summary is complete without some nod to the future. When we look at microlearning, it's clearly not going away, and it's also clear that other technologies are being called into service for microlearning.

We've already seen instances where virtual reality (VR) is used for microlearning. VR is a technology accessed via a headset, where the leaner dons goggles and is instantly transported to a realistic 3-D environment.

Since the goggles track to the learner's head and the images of the environment are all they see, the learner feels as if they are actually immersed in that environment.

In one instance of VR microlearning, vice presidents of a company were recorded answering specific questions that arose within the organization related to thinking at the enterprise level rather than at the departmental level. The recordings lasted between three and four minutes, providing either a story of how they tackled a problem or questions the senior manager could ask themselves or employees to help move toward a decision. Then they set up VR spaces for the senior managers to both "get away and reflect" and to jump into the VR. The "get away" aspect of VR felt like a one-on-one meeting, and because it was short the senior managers would be more likely to partake. The organization used VR because it wanted the senior managers to have an immersive, contextualized feeling, which created an environment and atmosphere that mimicked a common setting for the managers. This VR microlearning pilot was highly successful, and the company is expanding the program. It's just one example of how microlearning can be used with almost any technology.

Another huge expansion area for microlearning is augmented reality (AR), which is when a layer of images or words is placed in front of the learner through some technology. Once of the best examples is the Pokémon GO game, in which the player holds up their phone and can "see" Pokémon in the front yard, even though they aren't really there. Another good example is a car's heads up display, which projects turn-by-turn instructions on the windshield. This type of technology seems highly promising for microlearning, especially in the performance area, because it can provide step-by-step overlays of instructions. Technology is even moving toward embedding that into everyday eyeglasses, making it accessible to nearly everyone.

VR and AR are just two examples of how microlearning can leverage new-wave technology. We are sure that there will be many more instances of microlearning integrated with new technologies, standards for designing microlearning, and instructional foundations.

Short and Sweet

We've covered a great deal in *Microlearning: Short and Sweet* but this won't work without you. You now have the tools and techniques you need to be successful. This isn't the end of your journey to learn more about microlearning. It is just the start—the next step is all yours.

- Take what you have learned and apply it to your organization.
- Create a plan to implement microlearning into your learning initiatives and start the process.
- Design engaging, exciting microlearning pieces focused on the desired learning outcome.

References

Anderson, L.W., and D.R. Krathwohl. 2001. *A Taxonomy for Learning, Teaching, and Assessing*, Abridged Edition. Boston: Allyn and Bacon.

Armstrong, R.J. 1970. *Developing and Writing Behavioral Objectives.* Tucson, AZ: Educational Innovators Press.

Bandura, A., D. Ross, and S.A. Ross. 1961. "Transmission of Aggression Through the Imitation of Aggressive Models." *Journal of Abnormal and Social Psychology* 63(3): 575–582.

Bixler, B. 2007. "Psychomotor Domain Taxonomy." http://users.rowan.edu/~cone/curriculum/psychomotor.htm.

Bjork. 2012. "1. Retrieval as a Memory Modifier." Bjork Learning and Forgetting Lab. https://bjorklab.psych.ucla.edu/research/#itemI.

Brown, A.H., and T.D. Green. 2011. *The Essentials of Instructional Design: Connecting Fundamental Principles With Process and Practice,* 2nd ed. New York: Pearson.

Burns, R.A. 1985. "Information Impact and Factors Affecting Recall (Report No. ED258639)." Paper presented at the Annual National Conference on Teaching Excellence and Conference of Administrators. Austin, Texas, May 22–25.

Carpenter, S.K. 2014. "Spacing and Interleaving of Study and Practice." In *Applying Science of Learning in Education: Infusing Psychological Science Into the Curriculum,* edited by V.A. Benassi, C.E. Overson, and C.M. Hakala. Society for the Teaching of Psychology, http://teachpsych.org/ebooks/asle2014/index.php.

Carpenter, S.K., and E.L. DeLosh. 2005. "Application of the Testing and Spacing Effects to Name Learning." *Applied Cognitive Psychology* 19(5): 619–636.

Clark, R.C., and R.E. Mayer. 2011. *E-Learning and the Science of Instruction: Proven Guidelines for Consumers and Designers of Multimedia,* 3rd ed. San Francisco: Pfeiffer.

Dempster, F.N. 1987. "Effects of Variable Encoding and Spaced Presentations on Vocabulary Learning." *Journal of Educational Psychology* 79:162–170.

Dick, W., L. Carey, and J.O. Carey. 2009. *The Systematic Design of Instruction.* Upper Saddle River, NJ: Merrill/Pearson.

Dillon, JD. 2018. "Microlearning: The Ultimate Guide." Axonify, July 19. https://axonify.com/microlearning/#definition.

Dirksen, J. 2016. *Design for How People Learn,* 2nd ed. Berkeley, CA: New Riders.

Dobson, J.L. 2013. "Retrieval Practice Is an Efficient Method of Enhancing the Retention of Anatomy and Physiology Information." *Advances in Physiology Education* 37:184–191.

Downes, S. 2010. "New Technology Supporting Informal Learning." *Journal of Emerging Technologies in Web Intelligence* 2(1): 27–33.

Duffy, T.M., and D.H. Jonassen. 1992. *Constructivism and the Technology of Instruction: A Conversation.* Hillsdale, NJ: Lawrence Erlbaum Associates.

Ericsson, A., and R. Pool. 2016. *Peak: Secrets From the New Science of Expertise.* Boston: Houghton Mifflin Harcourt.

Finkenbinder, E.O. 1913. "The Curve of Forgetting." *The American Journal of Psychology* 24:8–32.

Friesens, N., and T. Hug. 2007. "Outline of a Microlearning Agenda." In *Didactics of Microlearning: Concepts, Discourses & Examples,* edited by T. Hug, 15–34. New York: Waxman.

Gates, A.I. 1917. "Recitation as a Factor in Memorizing." *Archives of Psychology* 6(40).

Gredler, M.E. 1997. *Learning and Instruction: Theory and Practice.* Upper Saddle River, NJ: Prentice-Hall.

Guo, P.J., J. Kim, and R. Rubin. 2014. "How Video Production Affects Student Engagement: An Empirical Study of MOOC Videos." ACM Conference on Learning at Scale. http://pgbovine.net/edX -video-production-research.htm.

Harvard University. 2013. "Online Learning: It's Different." ScienceDaily, April 4. www.sciencedaily.com/releases/2013/04/130404122240.htm.

Heller, O., W. Mack, J. Seitz. 1991. "Replikation der Ebbinghaus'schen Vergessenskurve mit der Ersparnis-methode: 'Das Behalten und Vergessen als Function der Zeit.'" Zeitschrift für Psychologie 199:3–18.

"Hermann Ebbinghaus." Wikipedia. https://en.wikipedia.org/w/index .php?title=Hermann_Ebbinghaus&oldid=888300069.

Hierdeis, H. 2007. "From Meno to Microlearning: A Historical Survey." In *Didactics of Microlearning,* edited by T. Hug, 35–52. New York: Waxmann.

Hodell, C. 2011. *ISD From the Ground Up,* 3rd ed. Alexandria, VA: ASTD Press.

Jonassen, D., M. Davidson, M. Collins, J. Campbell, and B.B. Haag. 1995. "Constructivism and Computer-Mediated Communication in Distance Education." *American Journal of Distance Education* 9(2): 7-26.

Kapp, K. 2003. *Winning E-Learning Proposals*. Boca Raton, FL: J. Ross Publishing.

Kerfoot, B.P. 2010. "Adaptive Spaced Education Improves Learning Efficiency: A Randomized Controlled Trial." *Journal of Urology* 183(2): 678–681.

Krathwohl, D.R., B.S. Bloom, and B.B. Masia. 1964. *Taxonomy of Educational Objectives: The Classification of Educational Goals. Handbook II: The Affective Domain*. New York: David McKay.

Landauer, T.K., and R.A. Bjork. 1978 "Optimal Rehearsal Patterns and Name Learning." In *Practical Aspects of Memory*, edited by M.M. Gruneberg, P.E. Morris, and R.N. Sykes. London: Academic Press, 625–632.

Lattuca, L.R., and J.S. Stark. 2009. *Shaping the College Curriculum: Academic Plans in Context*, 2nd ed. San Francisco: Jossey-Bass.

"Learning Taxonomy–Simpson's Psychomotor Domain." https://assessment.uconn.edu/wp-content/uploads/sites/1804/2016/06/LearningTaxonomy_Psychomotor.pdf

Long, A., B.P. Kerfoot, S. Chopra, T. Shaw. 2010. "Online Spaced Education to Supplement Live Courses." *Med Educ* 44:519–520.

mLevel. 2015. "IHG Case Study." mLevel.com. www.mlevel.com/blog/case-studies/ihg-case-study.

Murre, J.M.J., and J. Dros. 2015. "Replication and Analysis of Ebbinghaus' Forgetting Curve." *PLoS ONE* 10(7).

Pashler, H., D. Rohrer, N.J. Cepeda, and S.K. Carpenter. 2007. "Enhancing Learning and Retarding Forgetting: Choices and Consequences." *Psychon Bull Rev* 14(2): 187–193.

Radossawljewitsch, P.R. 1907. "Das Behalten und Vergessen bei Kindern und Erwachsenen nach experimentellen Untersuchungen" [An experimental investigation of the retention and forgetting among children and adults]. Leipzig: Nemnich.

Ramachandran, A., C. Snehalatha, J. Ram, S. Selvam, M. Simon, A. Nanditha, A.S. Shetty, I.F. Godsland, N. Chaturvedi, A. Majeed, N. Oliver, C. Toumazou, K.G. Alberti, and D.G. Johnston. 2013. "Efficacy of Mobile Phone Messaging in Prevention of Type 2 Diabetes by Lifestyle Change in Men at High Risk–A Randomised Clinical Trial in India." *Journal of Association of Physicians of India* 61.

Reider, L.P. 1994. *Computers, Graphics and Learning.* Madison, WI: Brown & Benchmark Publishers.

Rizzo, C.A. 2017. "Microlearning at John Hancock Investments Drives Results." *Learning Solutions,* October 9. www.learningsolutionsmag .com/articles/2466/microlearning-at-john-hancock-investments -drives-results.

Roediger, H.L., and J.D. Karpicke. 2006 "The Power of Testing Memory: Basic Research and Implications for Educational Practice." *Perspectives on Psychological Science* 1(3).

Russell, L. 2015. *Project Management for Trainers,* 2nd ed. Alexandria, VA: ATD Press.

Schank, R., and C. Cleary. 1995. *Engines for Education.* Evanston, IL: The Institute for Learning Sciences.

Shaw, T., A. Long, S. Chopra, B.P. Kerfoot. 2011. "Impact on Clinical Behavior of Face-to-Face Continuing Medical Education Blended With Online Spaced Education: A Randomized Controlled Trial." *J Contin Educ Health Prof* 31(2):103–108.

Siemens, G. 2005. "Connectivism: A Learning Theory for the Digital Age." *International Journal of Instructional Technology & Distance Learning* 2(1). www.itdl.org/journal/jan_05/article01.htm.

Thalheimer, W. 2017. "Definition of Microlearning." Work-Learning Research, January 13. www.worklearning.com/2017/01/13/definition- of-microlearning.

Thalheimer, W. 2018. "The Learning-Transfer Evaluation Model: Sending Messages to Enable Learning Effectiveness." Work-Learning Research. www.worklearning.com/wp-content/uploads/2018/02/Thalheimer-The-Learning-Transfer-Evaluation-Model-Report-for-LTEM-v11.pdf.

Tipton, S. 2017. "Microlearning: The Misunderstood Buzzword." LearningRebels.com, July 17. https://learningrebels.com/2017/07/17/microlearning-the-misunderstood-buzzword.

Torgerson, C. 2016. *The Microlearning Guide to Microlearning.* Torgerson Consulting.

Vlach, H.A., C.M. Sandhofer, and R.A. Bjork. 2014. "Equal Spacing and Expanding Schedules in Children's Categorization and Generalization." *Journal of Experimental Child Psychology* 123:129–137.

Westin, A. 2017. "Cost to Develop Microlearning?" E-Learning Heroes, June 5. https://community.articulate.com/discussions/building-better-courses/cost-to-develop-microlearning. Phil Mayor's comment on June 6, 2017.

About the Authors

Karl M. Kapp, EdD, is an international speaker, scholar, writer, and expert on the convergence of learning, technology, and business with a focus on game-thinking, games, and gamification for learning. He serves as a professor of instructional technology at Bloomsburg University in Bloomsburg, Pennsylvania, where he teaches several graduate courses and serves as the director of the university's Institute for Interactive Technologies. The institute works with businesses, nonprofits, and other organizations to help them create interactive and meaningful instruction.

Karl is an award-winning professor and author or co-author of eight books including the bestselling *The Gamification of Learning and Instruction* and *Play to Learn*. He is currently a senior researcher on a grant sponsored by the National Institutes of Health, which involves the intelligent use of microlearning. He also served as co-principle investigator on two National Science Foundation grants.

Karl is founder of the consulting and game development firm The Wisdom Learning Group, where he consults internationally with

Fortune 100 companies, government entities, and not-for-profits. On a sabbatical from Bloomsburg University, Karl completed a five-week tour of six different countries, where he studied the impact of games and play across cultures. He is now applying those insights to his current work.

Karl has received several industry awards, including the ATD Distinguished Contribution to Talent Development award, which honors those who have had a sustained impact on the talent development field. He was also named one of LinkedIn's Top Voices in Education in 2017 and received the eLearning Guild's honor of becoming a Guild Master in 2018. Karl has been a TEDx speaker and author of eight LinkedIn Learning courses including "Learning How to Increase Learner Engagement." He believes that play, creativity, and game-thinking leads to innovation, productivity, and profitability. Follow Karl on Twitter @kkapp.

Robyn A. Defelice, PhD, has served as a strategist and consultant in the learning and performance arena for more than 19 years. She also directs training initiatives for Revolve Solutions LLC, a service-disabled veteran-owned small business. She specializes in organizational learning management and convergence of decentralized training functions, reshaping learning organizations and operational frameworks for efficient, cost-effective sustainment of learning solutions. Her process focuses on total solution management and designing an infrastructure capable of maintaining current learning success while piloting and adopting new learning initiatives.

Robyn's a self-proclaimed geek for industry data that provides insight into the how, what, and why of learning and development. She is an advocate for learning and development teams and helping them understand their own challenges and capabilities for success.

As an adjunct professor with LaSalle University, Robyn teaches the art, science, and business of instructional design and the management of its learning and development projects. She also enjoys volunteering and mentoring emerging TD professionals from Bloomsburg University's instructional technology program, of which she is a proud alum.

Robyn's portfolio includes a range of industries and sectors, including major health and insurance systems and pharmaceutical sales, research, and manufacturing. She has also assisted multiple startups, higher education departments, and state and government agencies and programs.

Index

A

activities for reinforcing learning, 12
affective learning domain, 33–36
Aldrich, Clark, 127
American Society of Civil Engineers
    (ASCE)
    experiences implementing a
        microlearning strategy, 72–74
    learner motivation, 79
Anderson, Lorin, 30–31
attitudes, teaching and influencing
    celebrity endorsements, 35
    music's effect on, 36
    within organizations, 33–34
    testimonials, 35–36
augmented reality (AR), 169–170
Axonify microlearning platform,
    138–139

B

Bacon, Sir Francis, 63
Bandura, Albert, 24
Bee Naturals case study
    pensive microlearning, 44–45
    performance microlearning, 46–47
    persuasive microlearning, 47–48

post-instruction microlearning, 48–49
practice-based microlearning, 50
preparatory microlearning, 51–52
behavior
    continuing medical education
        example of spaced education's
        effect on, 63–64
    spacing effect's impact on, 63–64
behaviorism learning theory, 22–23
Bloom's Taxonomy, 30–31
breaking learning into microlearning
    segments, 12, 15–16, 124
Burns, Ralph, 65

C

change
    onboarding program example of a
        small change with a big impact
        on resources, 98–99, 100–101
    and risk, 97–98
Clark, Ruth, 117
classical conditioning, 22
cognitive learning domain, 30–33
cognitivism learning theory, 23–25
connectivism learning theory, 27–29

constructivism learning theory, 26–27
content
    curriculum, 76–79
    having a maintenance plan for, 99–101
    microlearning *vs.* traditional courses, 75
context switching, 44

D

Dave, RH, 37
Defelice, Robyn A., 80–81, 82
defining microlearning
    authors' definition, 11
    expert opinions, 9–10
    necessary elements of microlearning,
        11–13
    what microlearning is not, 13–17
Dempster, Frank, 62
Design for How People Learn (Dirksen), 79
designing microlearning
    gamification, 126–127
    graphic layout and aesthetics,
        121–123
    intentionally, 12, 16, 124
    key takeaways, 132–135
    NBC Universal (NBCU) example
        of matching microlearning
        design with need, 49, 110–113
    optimal length of a microlearning
        lesson, 65–66
    podcasting, 119–121
    for the psychomotor domain, 38
    short sims, 127–129
    storyboarding, 129–132
    three core concepts for developing a
        microlearning strategy, 74–76
    using sound design principles,
        113–114

video, 123–126
    writing style, 114–119
Dewey, John, 26
Didactics of Microlearning (Hug), 9–10
Dillon, JD, 10
Dirksen, Julie, 79
Downes, Stephen, 27

E

Ebbinghaus, Hermann, 57–59, 165
Ebbinghaus Forgetting Curve, 57–59,
    165
Electronic Performance Support Systems
    (Gery), 13
Elevate app for fundamental skills, 80–82
engagement
    brief, 11
    methods of, 11–12
    optimal length of a microlearning
        lesson, 65–66
Engines for Education (Schank), 43–44
Ericsson, Anders, 49
estimating microlearning development
    hours
    bottom-up estimation (work
        breakdown structure), 104–105
    comparing previous similar projects,
        102–103
    critical factors for, 101–102
    difficulty of, 106
    industry standards, 105–106
    setup cost, 103, 105
    weighted factor formulas
        (Parametric modeling), 103–104
    when using a template-driven
        microlearning tool, 106
evaluating microlearning training

compliance department example,
142–144, 145, 147, 150–152

effectiveness of the products and the
process, 96–97, 149–151

evaluation models, 144–149

evaluation planning, 100–101, 168

four factors for evaluation
(cost, resources, processes,
sustainment), 152–154

gathering information over time, 148

John Hancock Investments
example, 138–141

Kirkpatrick-Katzell four levels of
evaluation, 144–149

questions to ask about the
evaluation process, 142–144

SWOT (strengths, weaknesses, opportunities, threats) analysis, 149–152

using dashboards to access data
easily and in real-time, 140–141

examples of microlearning in action

Ashley and Nancy's flashcards for remembering terms, 7–8, 17–18, 23

diabetes healthier living habits
education, 4, 25, 47, 63

Intercontinental Hotels Group
employee training using
gamification, 4–5

Jane's short video to recall return
procedures, 7, 28–29, 45–46

Juan's educational app with daily
quizzes, 6–7, 15

Exponential Organizations (Ismail), 139

F

failure

Failco example of unsuccessful microlearning implementation, 90–93

formal learning

compared to informal learning, 83–84

potential limitations of, 85

formal *vs.* informal integration of
microlearning, 17–19

four factors for evaluation (cost, resources,
processes, sustainment), 152–154

future of microlearning

augmented reality (AR), 169–170

virtual reality (VR), 168–169

G

Gameffective platform, 160–161

gamification

game elements and their use, 126–127

Gameffective platform, 160–161

Intercontinental Hotels Group's use of
mLevel for employee training, 4–5

mLevel gamified platform, 4–5

structural gamification, 126

*The Gamification of Learning and
Instruction* (Kapp), 126

Gates, I., 63

Gery, Gloria, 13

graphics and visual design

charts and graphs, 122–123

flowcharts, 123

knowing when to use graphics,
121–122

selecting the most appropriate
images, 122

Guo, Philip, 65–66, 123–124

H

Hierdeis, Helmwart, 9–10
history of microlearning
flashcards, 13
from the perspective of performance
support, 13
sharable content object (SCO), 14
Skinner's programmed instruction
format, 23
the term microlearning, 56
unchanging nature of learning in
general, 157–158
before written language, 13–14
Hug, Theo, 9–10, 17

I

"Impact on Clinical Behavior of
Face-to-Face Continuing Medical
Education Blended with Online
Spaced Education" (study), 63–64
implementing microlearning. *See* planning and implementing microlearning
informal learning
benefits of, 85
compared to formal learning, 83–84
instructional design principles, 24–25
instructional unit, 11
intentional design of microlearning, 12,
16, 124
Ismail, Salim, 139

K

Kapp, Karl M., 126, 167
Karpicke, Jeffrey D., 63
Katzell, Raymond, 145
key performance indicator (KPI), 77
Kirkpatrick, Donald, 145

Kirkpatrick, Jim, 145
Kirkpatrick, Wendy, 145
Kirkpatrick-Katzell four levels of
evaluation, 144–149
Krathwohl, David, 30–31, 34

L

learning domains, 29–30
affective, 33–36
cognitive, 30–33
psychomotor, 36–39
push or pull delivery to the learner,
83–86
understanding the importance of, 165
learning ecosystem
macro, meso, and micro levels of
learning, 9–10, 17–19
microlearning as part of the, 14, 17
skill development, 15
learning methods
comparing formal *vs.* informal, 83–86
Mary example of selecting both
push and pull learning, 84–85
learning theories
behaviorism, 22–23
cognitivism, 23–25
connectivism, 27–29
constructivism, 26–27
social cognitive theory (SCT), 24
understanding the importance of, 165

M

macro, meso, and micro levels of
learning, 9–10, 17–19
Mayer, John, 117
Mayor, Phil, 105

measuring the effectiveness of
microlearning. *See* evaluating
microlearning training
memory
Ebbinghaus Forgetting Curve, 57–59
mass practice (cramming), 60
recall, 62–63
spacing effect, 60–64
testing for aiding retention, 62–63
*Memory: A Contribution to Experimental
Psychology* (Ebbinghaus), 57
*The Microlearning Guide to
Microlearning* (Torgerson), 9
microlearning map, 76–79, 82, 86
mLevel gamified platform, 4–5
motivation
adding a motivational element to
the microlearning map, 82
American Society of Civil Engineers
(ASCE) example, 79
expectation setting, 79–81
self-control, 80–81
self-efficacy, 79–81
as a want *vs.* as a need, 79

O

operant conditioning, 22
outcomes of microlearning, 12–13

P

Parametric modeling, 103–104
participants in microlearning
focus on performance instead of
learning, 13, 16, 46
in the psychomotor domain, 38–39
Pavlov's dogs example of classical
conditioning, 22
Piaget, Jean, 26

planning and implementing
microlearning
52 educational emails example, 95–96
adding new activities for companies already providing microlearning, 93
evaluation planning, 100–101
Failco example of unsuccessful
implementation, 90–93
implementation activities, 95
importance of proper planning,
89–90, 92–93
Payoneer example of using
microlearning and gamification
on a daily basis, 158–162
pilot testing, 95–96
production stages
1–pre-production, 94–95, 124
2–production, 95–96
3–post-production, 96–97
risk and change management, 97–99
storyboarding, 129–132
sustainment and maintenance of
content, 99–101
podcasting
audio considerations, 119–120
benefits of, 119
introducing content, 120–121
recording equipment, 120
"The Power of Testing Memory Basic
Research and Implications for
Educational Practice" (paper), 63
Presentr practice-based microlearning
app, 49, 110–113
Project Management for Trainers
(Russell), 103–104
psychomotor learning domain, 36–39
push *vs.* pull delivery of learning, 83–86

R

research on microlearning
    applicability of experiments to the real world, 58–59
    Ebbinghaus Forgetting Curve, 57–59, 165
    keeping up with, 166
    optimal length of a microlearning lesson, 65–66
    recall, 62–63
    spacing content, 61–64
resource libraries, 14–15
retrieval
    the act of retrieving information as a learning event, 61, 62
    spaced retrieval, 61
    testing as an effective way of learning, 62–63
risk
    the balance between low and high risk, 98
    and change, 97–98
    onboarding program example of a small change with a big impact on resources, 98–99, 100–101
Rizzo, Charles A., 138–141
Roediger, Henry L., III, 63
Rothnie, Neomie, 162
Russell, Lou, 103–104

S

Schank, Roger, 43–44
short sims
    benefits of, 127–129
    developing, 129
    goal of, 128
Siemens, George, 27–28
Skinner, B.F., 22–23

social cognitive theory (SCT), 24
storyboarding
    benefits of, 129–130
    creating a table of the script, blocking, and digital assets used, 130–132
strategies for implementing microlearning
    American Society of Civil Engineers (ASCE) example, 72–74
    civil engineering example of a microlearning map, 77–79, 82, 86
    developing a plan, 166–167
    formal vs. informal learning, 82–86
    making a microlearning map, 76–79, 82, 86
    necessary components, 74, 87
    three core concepts, 74–76
Sullenberger, Chesley ("Sully"), 15
sustainment and maintenance of content, 99–101
SWOT (strengths, weaknesses, opportunities, threats) analysis, 149–152

T

Thalheimer, Will, 10
time
    and engagement, 65–66
    estimating the time it takes to develop microlearning, 101–106
    ideal spacing between learning events, 61–62
    optimal length of a microlearning lesson, 65–66
Tipton, Shannon, 9
Torgerson, Carla, 9
types of microlearning
    determining which type to use, 163–165

pensive, 43–45, 163
performance-based, 45–47, 163–165
persuasive, 47–48, 164
post-instruction, 48–49, 164
practice-based, 49–50, 164
preparatory, 51–52, 164

U

use cases for microlearning
    about, 41–42
    considerations for the microlearning
        initiative, 42–43
    determining which use case is most
        appropriate, 52–53
    pensive, 43–45
    performance-based, 45–47
    persuasive, 47–48
    post-instruction, 48–49
    practice-based, 49–50
    preparatory, 51–52
    use case design worksheet, 52–53

V

video
    advantages of informal videos,
        124–125
    avoiding classroom settings, 124
    best practices, 123–125
    explainer (whiteboard)
        microlearning, 125–126
    instructor style, 124
virtual reality (VR), 168–169
Vygotsky, Lev, 26

W

work breakdown structure (WBS) for
    estimating, 104–105

writing style
    active voice, 116–117
    balance between formal and
        informal tone, 116–117
    concise scripting, 114–116, 167
    creating good microlearning
        questions, 117–119
    forward scheduling question
        example, 118
    Keep It Short and Simple (K-I-S-S),
        114–115, 121–122
    three-step outline, 115–116

Z

zone of proximal development, 26